THE LADY SPY

and

CON MAN

by

Dr. Gerald A. Walford

DISCLAIMER

THIS IS NOT A TRUE STORY, BUT IT IS BASED ON TRUE FACTS. THE CONS AND SCAMS FOUND WITHIN THIS BOOK DID OCCUR IN REAL LIFE. BREHTT BENNET IS A FICTITIOUS CON MAN, AND NATASHA ROMANSKI IS A FICTIOUS SPY. THE CONS AND SPYING IN THIS NARRATIVE HAVE BEEN CARRIED OUT THROUGH THE YEARS BY OTHER PEOPLE.

ACKNOWLEDGMENTS

Claude L. Crum Ph.D. was instrumental in editing this book. His experience as an English Professor and College Dean was most helpful in the organization of the book as well as the grammar and syntax.

As I see it, the thing you gotta do is eliminate the risk beforehand; make sure you're gonna win before you put down a bet.

Alvin Clarence Thomas – alias Titanic Thompson

PUBLISHED BOOKS by Dr. Gerald A. Walford

Biography:
CONTROLLING ADVERSITY.

Baseball/softball:
THE BASEBALL/SOFTBALL SWING OF THE FUTURE.

Concentration:
CONCENTRATION AND OTHER MENTAL SKILLS FOR SPORTS, LIFE AND THE ARTS.

E-books amazon:
HOW TO WRITE A BOOK.
KARATE CHOP GOLF.

Golf: (Class A - Professional Golfers' Association of America). THE GOLF SUPERBOOK (700 page book).
 SLAPSHOT GOLF - learning golf through the hockey slapshot and baseball swing.
THE GOLF WHISPERER.
PERFORMANCE GOLF.
GOLF'S POWER SECRETS.
PRACTICAL GOLF COACHING MANUAL for the World Golf Teachers Federation.

History:
SPORT, RELIGION AND WAR – Through the Ages

Hockey:
COACHING GIRLS ICE HOCKEY.
COACHING HOCKEY.
HOCKEY SKILLS.
YOUTH HOCKEY.

ICE HOCKEY - AN ILLUSTRATED GUIDE.

Humor: Major area of Ph.D. study.
HUMOR AND PERSONALITY.
SPORT HUMOR.

Humor, Psychology And Medical:
I MAY BE CRAZY BUT I AM NOT STUPID – The Life of a Mental
Patient on the PGA Tour

leadership:
DETERMINING THE FUTURE THROUGH LEADERSHIP SKILLS.

Mystery Novel:
THE LADY SPY AND CON MAN

Psychology:
PSYCHOPATHS and SOCIOPATHS and ANTISOCIAL BEHAVIOR

Teaching:
THE TAO OF TEACHING.

The life of the spy and the con man is very similar.

Both live a risky and dangerous life.
Both are after the money.
Both do extensive planning in their play.
Both understand the behavior of people.
Both are like psychologists.
Both are influential in talk and actions.
Both are risk takers.
Both are daring in life and work.
Both may have some psychopath tendencies.
Both have little concern for others.
Both are liars
Both can role-play like actors/actresses depending upon
the situation.

THE LADY SPY AND CON MAN

CHARACTERS
Natasha Romanski: agent 06 Russian underworld.
Mark O'Dell: first target. Businessman.
Stella Pearson: second target. CEO at AdMan Advertising agency.
Ralph Pearson: spouse to Stella. CIA agent.
Brehtt Bennett: Natasha's twin. The con man.
Jim Sloan: senator from Arizona, vying for the next presidency.
Kelly Sloan: Jim's wife.
Dr. Bill Sullivan: the neurologist at Washington City Hospital.

CHAPTER 1

THE SPY LADY

Natasha steps out of the tub. The warm water is dripping off her nude body. She looks at her bathtub partner, "It was a nice evening. I hope we can do it again. It is late and I must go."

She is at the end of the tub, dripping water on the floor. She is facing the beautiful lady in the tub and locks eyes on her. She leans over and places her hands on her knees. With slow and gentle caresses, her hands slide along the thighs of the woman, lying on her back, legs spread in giving her vagina a temptation to Natasha.

"Oh, you sweet thing," as Natasha slowly moves her hands in slow caresses towards the lady's vagina. The lady closes her eyes and squirms, expecting the kiss of love on and in her vagina. She is dreaming of Natasha's lips with high expectations.

Natasha's hands nears her lover's vagina and then slide back down to her knees. She rubs the knees and then slides her hands under the kneecaps of the bent legs. With a strong pull on the legs towards her body, her lover gasps for air with a quick powerful inhaling action. As she gasps, her body is pulled under the water level and her inhaling action pulls in the bubble bath water into her lungs. She drowns.

Natasha dries her body and wipes the dripping water from the floor where she was standing and all around the tub area. Water left on the floor may indicate someone was with the lady in the tub. She gets dressed and leaves.

She reflects, "The police will assume she drowned by falling asleep in the warm water and gradually slipping down into the water. There is no sign of force or violence. Athletes have been known to drown while in whirlpools. As they become excessively relaxed from the swirling hot water, they fall asleep and just slide down under the water. Hot tubs have also claimed their victims the same way."

Just as Natasha had predicted, the police declared the same assumption. Natasha has met her assignment. The only regret she has is that she does not know why the lady had to be killed. The killing did not bother her, but she laments on losing a wonderful sex partner.

She sleeps in late the next morning, as it is the natural thing to do when you are out all night. When sleeping in there is no need for an alarm clock. She is wealthy so she pampers herself. In her line of work, it is an asset. She works out in the gym and spa to keep that perfect body for athletic performance and for visual shape to please the men and yes the women also. Why not! She loves them both, men and women, physically, emotionally, and visually. Why not? A kiss is a kiss, lips to lips, tongue to tongue. Close your eyes. Can you tell the difference? Only if he hasn't shaved or if the smell is cologne or perfume. What if the kiss, licking and sucking is on the breast or genitalia? With the eyes closed it feels good, wonderful and even out of this world. A penis or a woman's tongue makes no difference to Natasha Romanski. It is sex, just sex and this is why she loves her job so much.

Her appearance helps her attract people. She is tall, five feet, eleven inches in her sneakers. In high heels her beautiful head is above most people so she is easily noticed. Her hair is naturally blond, somewhat short in perhaps a masculine way. Her body is long, thin and considered aerodynamically shaped in that her breasts are small. Her legs are long and strong to give her an athletic and perhaps even a slight androgynous appearance. Despite her small breasts, she is still an extremely beautiful woman. A woman of class. A Nordic goddess. A goddess who does not try to be sexy and alluring. She just is.

To get information or to complete an assignment she is encouraged to use the power of sex on men and women. She was trained for 18 months in how to accomplish her assignments and for 3 months in how to use the most powerful aphrodisiac of sex on people. She learned to read bodies, body language, and how to use her body and eyes to entice and lure people to her lair. She learned the subtle use of the right words at the right time and how to coordinate it with her body language. She learned how to breathe, hold her breath, and exhale to accentuate her cleavage to stop a man's breath cycle. She learned how to touch or caress her target at the appropriate time to begin the seduction and carry it to completion. Her teachers would take her out for fieldwork where they would watch the people go by and the teacher would pick a target, man, women, or teenager and tell her to seduce the target. Sometimes she would be given a time limit like, "That person. You have 30 minutes to seduce the target, get his phone, address, marital status, and work address."

This she loved. Why not? If she was good she could get more sex, every day and several times a day. On her 30-minute assignments, she would lure the target into an alley, an isolated park bench, a car, behind a tree and sometimes in the back of a bus or commuter train.

She loved it because she got what she wanted most, money and sex, not necessarily in that order. Her agency, as it was referred to in an attempt to sound legitimate and legal, knew how to pick their workers, young, good looking, energetic and athletic. The same requirement for men and women. However, the agency was smart as they were well aware that in most cases women had the advantage over men in obtaining information. Men could work on the women and men but their ability with the men was limited unless the target was homosexual. If the target was homosexual then the agent also had to play the 'homo' whether he liked it or not. In such cases, the man gets a financial bonus, however most were never assigned to 'homos'. Only a few wanted that privilege.

Does the agency have a name? Not really, it is just part of the Russian government. When information or other action is needed, the agent is notified and not necessarily by a superior because the agent does no know who the superior is. For example, the head of defense could contact her for an assignment. The head of finance could also do the same. It seems like a slip-shod procedure, but it does work and it leaves no trail. Agents are notified by a hand printed assignment, which must be burned immediately after reading. Good memory is essential. No computers or typewriters are used, as messages on a computer can still be in the computer somewhere even if the message is deleted. Typewriters have also been traced by the characteristics of their print. The agency is meticulous in no trails being left. They are so good that even the world powers are not aware of this agency. If an agent errs, the error is not traceable. Suspicion may occur but there is no real hard evidence. Natasha has good security. She feels safe, happy, financially secure and she gets to fuck all she wants. It's a great life.

THE CON MAN

He gets out of his BMW, locks the car remotely and proceeds to the Blue Fox Night Club. He steps inside, looks around and sees little action. To him the place is dead. He greets the bartender with familiarity as he knows them all.

"Little dead tonight, Al?"

"Yeah, may pick up later, but who knows? One of those days."

"I may come back later. See ya."

He walks back to his car, looks around and sees some people walking to the club up the street.

>Yeah, just maybe I will try it up there.

Leaving his car, he walks to the new club with high expectations.

>"I need help. I'm suffering with blue balls – well actually, I have navy blue balls. I don't care what she looks like, well . . . I do have standards but the color of my balls often lowers my standards. At pink, my standards are extremely high. At blue, my standards are relatively high. At navy blue, my standards are medium. At black, my standards are so low I just hope she or it is human.

He walks up to the gate, a heavy doored entrance guarded by the bouncer. A careless scrutiny by the bouncer determines he is over 18, physically - mentally doesn't count.

He enters and like all men, horney and half-horney men, he scans the large lounge area. His face reveals a satisfied look. Prospects look good. He proceeds to the center area and notices an attractive woman, late twenties or early thirties. In bars and lounges the weak lighting makes women look younger.

"Let's not be concerned about age. My need is greater than my age requirements."

With no hesitation but with strong confidence he approaches her despite the fact that her back is to him. When he reaches her, he sidesteps and walks past to be in front of her.

"Best to never come up from behind a woman. Such procedures can startle or even scare them. A scared woman is not a receptive woman."

As he is now in front of her, he turns his head to look over his shoulder, looks right at her and into her eyes and with a smile he utters the classic pick-up line, "Hi."

His friendly face works and she responds with "Hi, how are you?"

"Oh, I was neutral until I passed you, and now that I looked back over my shoulder I progressed to extremely good."

She blushes. The line was a little corny but appreciated and so she thanks him for the compliment.

"I would like to talk further with you. Can I bring you a drink?"

"I would like one but I am leaving."

He now notices a slight grin to her smile and a twinkle in her eyes.

"Perhaps next time I see you." As he speaks, he feels a little uncomfortable but does not know why. Looking into her eyes, he sees her eyes change focus from his eyes to just over his shoulder. Oh, oh… he turns his head to the side to see a giant, six foot seven, about 285 lbs, bent over so he is eyeball to eyeball, with noses almost touching, he grins and the giant.

"This is my boyfriend. He plays for the New York Jets, middle linebacker."

"I, errr . . . ha . . . I do admire your taste in women." A statement he knows will go unanswered.

The giant moves straight forward towards his girlfriend while pushing him aside.

There is no way he will challenge a confrontation. Discretion is the better part of valor. Ah, to save face.

Never let a set back or defeat stop progress. There is now one less woman to try. He moves on, scanning the room. Tactics change as he sees three women huddled together in laughing mode.

This he likes as women like to travel in pairs or groups. Maybe this is from evolutionary growth patterns as women are much less strong than men and felt more protected and safer when grouped.

As he approaches, he determines his target, or his first choice. He realizes that there is a possibility that he could end up with two or if really good or lucky, all three but let's not get greedy.

> *"Now the trick is to approach the second and third choices of the three and not the prime target. By showing interest in the two non-targets and a lack of interest in the prime target, the prime target will feel isolated and ignored. With this feeling, the prime target will be assertive in getting to be noticed and part of the male's attention."*

> *"Women are competitive. Do not be told otherwise. In love, sex, relationships, courtship, etc. women are competitive – big time. They want the best boyfriend, and the best looking male, the richest or wealthiest alpha dog so the others, especially women, will notice. Women get upset if they spend money and time for the best-looking*

dress to outdo the others. They will be upset if someone else shows up in the same dress. Is this not competitive?"

"My objective now is to be totally different than any other wolves using the same, trite, and boring opening lines. I must not look like I'm on the prowl, just a friendly passing by comment."

He walks toward them and as he passes he looks and asks, "You guys know the weather for tomorrow? I got a big golf tournament so I would like to prepare for good or bad weather." He does not stop but slowly back pedals looking and waiting for an answer.

"It's going to rain so bring your umbrella, rain suits and goulashes with spikes," they respond with a few giggles and friendly smiles.

"With spikes, eh. Sounds like you guys know your golf."

"We play a little, but not tomorrow."

The backpedaling stops and he moves to the group, as they seem receptive. He positions himself facing the second and third choices with his back partially facing his desired target. The talk continues about their golf games, but the prime target feels left out and ignored so she breaks in with a comment about her game and her problem with sand traps. The prime target is now competing with her two friends for attention and she gets it.

Slowly turning to face the prime, he turns, faces her and apologizes for his rude behavior of ignoring her. She smiles and the game is on. He then looks, almost stares, into her eyes and says, "Hi, my name is Brehtt Bennett. And yours is . . .

"Cemone Harris."

"What a lovely name." He then turns to the other two and utters, "Are your names as lovely?" as he extends his hand after his flattery comment.

"I'm Betty." "I'm Noreen."

Now that the ice is broken, they talk of everything until closing time is near. Betty and Noreen rise to go to the rest room while Cemone stays so Brehtt is not left alone. Time is running out so Brehtt makes his pitch for the rest of the night. She accepts and when her friends return she bids them farewell and leaves with Brehtt.

Betty says to Noreen, "Is Cemone working on her slut skills?"

"Yeah, and I think we better brush up on ours."

"Definitely."

Brehtt and Cemone drive to his apartment. The car is parked and they advance to his apartment. Once inside they sit on the sofa. They talk, kiss a little, and fully embrace each other. "Cemone, I am not interested in fucking you now. I would like to know you better. So how 'bout if we just talk with a few kisses and hugs. I do not like to get too involved on the first date,"

"Okay."

CHAPTER 2

THE SPY LADY

She is in her luxurious apartment reading her assignment, which she reads several times, studying and memorizing the information. The photos of her target are from several angles so a complete identity can be made no matter the angle or situation of the target. In a short time, she remembers all the data and photos. She then gets up, burns them in her fireplace and then spreads the ashes around to make sure all is burned.

She then proceeds to her bathroom, removes her workout clothes and showers. She then proceeds to apply makeup, hairstyle and perfume to her neck, breast, and genitals. After all, her assigned target may just like the sweet smell as he explores her body. These procedures excite her, as she knows what comes next. Besides, her target looks kind of appealing, fairly tall, well groomed, and slender with no potbelly. Once she is ready, she looks into the full-length mirror to appraise herself and while looking to also admire herself. "Shit girl you are ready."

She walks to her door, presses the buttons for her alarm system, closes the door and proceeds to the elevator for the ground floor parking lot. She approaches her car, a Lamborghini, what else would such a high-class lady have? A Chevy would just not do, so bourgeoisie. She clicks the remote and the car opens. She slides in and smells the new car atmosphere. After all, she always gets that smell because she gets a new one every year. She buckles up and scoots out to the street, into traffic and to the bar where her target goes for his "happy hour" treat to impress himself and his buddies with his important work, his value to society and his grandiose personality.

As Natasha drives to the bar of the Holiday Inn, she feels quite secure in this affair. She does not know why or the reasons for what she has to do.

She is paid big bucks for not knowing and just doing. Again, no paper trails or police investigations for mistakes.

She parks and walks into the hotel, but she does not just walk, she sashays, she sways the hips, her head is up, straight ahead with her eyes covered with large sunglasses that seem to cover half her face. The hiding of the eyes. The creation in the mystery of what's behind the glasses. She reaches the entrance. The doorman tucks in his belly, a trait many men do on nearing a beautiful woman. He opens the door but his face is blushing red from tucking in his belly as his breath diminishes. He hopes she moves in quickly so he can breathe again. She does and she heads straight to the lounge, picks a small table for two, sits down and scans the crowd for her target. He should easily be found as his personality description in the file says he works at being the center of attention.

There he was, as expected in the center of the bar, laughing loudly and talking loudly with grandiose body movements. From his photos, she was somewhat impressed and looking forward to a "Romp in the hay" but now she simply had a job to do as this guy was too much of himself.

She knew how to get this guy. It would be easy. She would not have to leave her table and chair. Mr. Hot Shot would soon scan the crowd, look for a woman, and excuse himself from the group. He would have to excuse himself so these buddies would know he was on the make and walking towards a woman. This was his ego builder, *"I'm a stud"*.

Natasha just looked at him and as he scanned the crowd, their eyes locked, she smiled and he then did the excusing of himself to his group so they could see him proceed to the girl. As he proceeded to Natasha, his friends made snide remarks and derogatory comments, which he could not hear. Anyway, he made it to the table sat down with no courtesy of asking if he may join and opened with the brilliant come on of "My name is Mark, and is your name as beautiful as your body."

"My name is Rose."

"Well, how are you. Did you have a good day?"

"No, it is a bad day. I am going to have a drink and then I am going to the spa for a massage in the hope I can have a relaxing evening."

"Oh, baby. I can save you money. I can give you a massage and fix you up for the most relaxing evening and night you ever had."

"Sounds like you're all talk."

"I am good! Try me!"

"OK."

They get up. She slips her hand into his elbow and they walk out. He registers for a room and they proceed to the elevator. The ride up to the 11th floor was terrible. He made a pass on feeling her bum. She froze, but did nothing. *Let's get this over with.* The pawing continued from the bum to the breast to the 11th floor. They walked to the room. He closed the door and started to take her clothes off. Clumsily he worked on her blouse and ripped the buttons. He grabbed her by the waist and back peddled her to the bed and dumped her there. Jumped on top of her and then tried to take her clothes off and his. His mouth slobbered all over her face.

Now she was irritated. She yells at him, "Let's get up and take our clothes off, have a drink in the nude and then get down to business.

"OK. Sounds like a good idea"

"You get the bed ready. I will play bartender, Open the drinks from the in-room bar and give you a nude bartender serving from the titty bar. You like that."

"Yeahhhhh.

"Get in bed so I can serve you."

She gets the drinks, unnoticed by the target because she was trained and was good with hand manipulation or sleight of hand as they say in the trade, she slips her assassin pill into his drink. He gulps the drink down in one swig, tosses the glass to the floor, grabs her and dumps her on the bed, gets on top to repeat where he was a few moments ago and starts pumping his hips. But nothing is happening. He feezes. "What's happening," he screams.

"Relax, honey. We just started too fast. Let me rub you like the massage you promised me."

"Shit. You really wanted a message?"

"Yes, I did, but you got me so excited with your manly ways that I wanted to fuck first."

"I know. I know what women want. I know they like it . . . I can't breathe. I. . ."

His body goes limp. His face is all squished from the pain. Eyes closed. His hands clutching his penis, after all it is his most prized possession even though he did not know how to use it.

Natasha looks at him, "Well this is one fucked up date. But, the assignment is done. Money in the bank in a couple of days when verification is made of his death."

THE CON MAN

Brehtt Bennett is a con man. His life involves taking from others. It can be money, sex, favors, or anything that he wants or needs. His experience has limits. He refuses to take from those who cannot afford the con. He knows that when he takes money it must not be money for kids, wife or family. His targets are people who can afford the con. Money cons vary to the wealth of the individual. In most cases when people are conned out of money they will not report the incident as it is too embarrassing. However, if the money is really high then the chances of being reported increase. As for sex, he tries to keep his cons in the single, divorced or separated range. Some husbands just will not accept such happenings, so why mess with the chance of private detectives putting him under surveillance. Why take chances when there are so many non-married women out there? Nevertheless, realistically, this rule is often broken.

Con artists are abundant in all races and cultures. Ironically, some cons are even liked. Remember the movie the STING with Paul Newman and Robert Redford. Two lovable con artists. It is remarkable that the con artist is loved when the sting is not on him or her because his thought process is how stupid the person was to be conned. In reality, it could have been him or her just as easily. In real life, we often admire the con artist for his daring and gutsy manipulation of people. It's a vicarious experience.

The con artist reflects the word "confidence" as the artist takes the mark into his confidence. The mark has confidence in the artist to do what he says he will do. If the artist cannot gain the mark's confidence, he leaves the mark for another one. The con involves trust. The more one can gain trust the easier it is to deceive the person. Trust is a double edge sword. In marriage, when one trusts a spouse the easier it is to cheat.

Brehtt is a super salesman. He can sell and could make a good living with honest sales, but there is no excitement or even danger to honest sales. The Con gives him power, a feeling of superiority over not only his mark but people in general. This feeling often gives the Con an indifference towards people. To the Con, people are stupid, and deserve to get what they get.

The con is a premier psychologist. His beliefs and personality change to fit the situation. He can be religious or atheist, happy or sad, helpful or mean. The con's personality is what is needed for the success of the con. Because of these traits, the con is an excellent actor capable of faking emotions needed at the time. The con has to fake the emotions because he usually does not have the emotions as he cares little for the mark or marks. He is for himself.

Brehtt is also a supreme athlete in striking skills like golf and baseball. He chose golf because he did not have to rely on teammates to win his money. His golf game was PGA Tour caliber but he did not ever try to qualify as he could make lots of money hustling. On tour he would be required to make starting times, practice times, etc. He just liked being free to move when he wanted. He did beat and win lots of money against PGA Tour players.

Many rich people, especially country club players, would take a crack at him, but few succeeded even when they were given strokes. Brehtt was just born with excellent eyesight and hand-eye coordination. These skills also helped in handgun, rifle, skeet, trap shooting and various pool games. These assets would give him the ability to play golf right and left-handed, which would provide the opportunity to up the wagers.

An interesting aspect of marks is that often they may suspect a con but just will not believe it. Some marks have been told it's a con but they just refuse to believe it. Lonely widows are often in this category and very vulnerable to con artists who love them, then take their money and leave.

Brehtt lies on his bed with all these thoughts racing through his mind. He must maintain these beliefs and not weaken. If he gets a mark, he must never feel sorry for the mark. Emotions must not enter into the picture. If he has empathy towards the mark, he must leave for someone else.

"No more reminiscing," he frowns. "Back to work."

CHAPTER 3

THE SPY LADY

At 8:35 am, she walks into her apartment and notices a pale blue envelop on the floor, picks it up, checks her answer machine and then turns on the TV. She sprawls out on her Lazy-boy. She is tired, up all night in her therapy session. That is what she calls it but it is often referred to as an orgy where swingers meet for conversation and sex.

". . . reporting on the death of Mark O'Dell in the Holiday Inn. O'Dell was found on his hotel room's disarrayed bed. It is believed he had a heart attack caused from the bottle of pills scattered on the floor and bed. So far the investigation suggests suicide. His co-workers claimed he was not too happy at work as the stress was talking its toll. Some information was leaked that he was involved with the Russian mob. Now for the weather . . . she clicks the remote.

"Tough luck you dumb shit. Now you cannot fuck up other women," she loudly mumbles. Her little anger alerts her to opening her pale blue envelope. She knows it's another job. "Boy, they not going to give me any rest. She opens it and gives it a quick scan and reads, *"Your assignment is Stella Pearson of the AdMan Agency. She is an executive officer and her husband is with the Central Intelligence Agency. Short forms are not used as all names are fully spelled out to prevent possible confusion. Photos of Stella are enclosed. She is beautiful and a bitch as several agents, men and women, have tried but cannot get past a hello. Her longest conversation with an agent was, "Yes, it is a nice day," and then she walks off. She is friendly to no one. She is not the real target. Her husband is. He is high up in the Central Intelligence Agency in the affairs of the Middle East with emphasis on military actions. He also has some dealings with the Ukraine. We need information on their knowledge so we can plan and plot counter measures. We need information and you are our best source. Others have failed but your success rate warrants you to the assignment. Sex as a measure to procure information may be difficult as she is one cold bitch. She and her husband have separate bedrooms. Neither have affairs with the opposite sex or the same sex. Each use the other as a trophy spouse as there are many advantages. This is a tough assignment. Use any means possible or available. You have unlimited budget. Good Luck."*

"Enough of this shit, I need sleep." She looks at the nightstand beside the bed with two dildo's and one vibrator all sitting perpendicular. She stares with wanton eyes, *"Fuck no, I can't take any more,"* jumps in bed, covers up and goes dead before her head hit the pillow.

1:23 pm she wakes up. Puts on shorts, tee shirt and jogging shoes, goes out the door to the street, and takes her 5-mile run. She feels good and the run is invigorating. She runs up the stairs instead of the elevator, into her apartment, strips and showers. A light breakfast of easy over eggs, toast and Canadian bacon with grape juice. Ahhh, now to review her new assignment.

She gets on the internet for Google Maps to locate the AdMan Advertising Agency and surrounding area and businesses. While studying the area she is plotting as to how best meet this lady. I must be slow and careful. She studies the main entrance, the steps leading to the main door, the doors leading in to a small vestibule and then another set of doors to the main entrance lobby.

Now that she knows the location, she dresses conservatively, with limited makeup. Out the door to her car but changes her mind and goes to the front door where the door attendant orders a taxi. When on assignment she does not like to use her own car as it may be recognized and is easily traceable.

She pays the taxi, gets out and surveys the area. A café, "The Quiky Lunch Café" is across the street with big windows. This looks like a good place to have coffee and do a stakeout of Stella leaving and going in. She then goes up the stairs, enters the door, through the vestibule and through the next door and into the main lobby. She stealthily walks around, scanning while trying to look unnoticeable. She soon gets the lay of the land and she then returns to go to The Quky Lunch Café. She enters and takes a quick left to a window table, sits and waits for service. She orders coffee and lemon pie to nibble on while a long wait is possible. It is now 3:35 pm.

At 4:13 pm, Stella comes out the main exit and hails a cab. Natasha makes note of time, in her little book. No information is left to chance. As Natasha watches Stella leave, she starts to formulate her plan. Normal circumstances would have her observe Stella's routing for a week, at least but her plan is to go tomorrow. The café is ideal for her waiting for the right time. She now goes home but stops for a little shopping at Victoria's Secret and Fredericks for that ideal charm piece of clothes and why not some new expensive perfume.

On entering her apartment, she goes through her routine of pale blue envelope, answer machine, TV and flopping onto the Lazy-boy. "*. . . no evidence of murder on the Mark O'Dell investigation. The case is being labeled as a suicide brought on by stress at work, divorce proceedings, DUI, driving under the influence, twice, and loss of driver's License. Connections to the Russian mob has revealed uncertainty. . .*" Click goes the remote and the TV goes black. "Fuck him."

She undresses and goes to bed. Picks up her book, "Fifty Shades of Grey."

At 9:30 am, she is out jogging. At this time, there is less traffic so the run is better. After the run, it is the usual routine again with shower, light snack, dress conservatively, little make up, get a taxi and go sit at the window table of the Quiky Café for her target. She orders a coffee to go and waits. At 4:25 pm, Stella rushes out the door. Natasha is crossing the street and moving to Stella. Stella raises her arm to hail a taxi. With the agility of an African lion, Natasha sweeps in as the arm is coming down and bumps into Stella. On contact, Natasha squeezes the Styrofoam cup, the lid pops off and spills a little on Stella's dress.

"You clumsy idiot, you spilled coffee on my dress."

Natasha's eyes go wide. She freezes with hand over mouth. "My God, I am so sorry, please forgive me; I must help you in any way possible."

"Yea, like a slutty bitch like you could afford a dress like this."

"Please forgive me," as she takes three five hundred dollar bills out of her purse and hands it to Stella.

Stella is caught off guard and surprised. Weakly she sputters, "It is not that much. Maybe dry cleaners may do."

Natasha makes her take the money. Now Stella is impressed. She is awed by how easily the girl gives up $1,500 dollars. She must be rich. She must have power. After all, Stella loves power as in her job and marriage to her CIA husband. Stella also loves money.

The anger is over and so Natasha in following through in her rushing actions hurries down the street to give the impression she was in a hurry. Natasha rushes away and says, "I hope we do not meet again."

With a sly smile and seeing the humor in the statement, Stella replies, "Same here." And they depart. One thinking, yes we will and the other thinking, I hope not.

THE CON MAN

BACK TO WORK

After all his reflections on his lifestyle, it's back to work, so he takes a nap. Whenever possible, after heavy thought on reflecting his scams, or in planning, he takes a nap. Research claims that having a nap, or sleeping overnight, after heavy skill learning or cognitive learning, causes the brain to keep working on the problems, and the brain often comes up with the solution during dreams or when awake the next day.

Jack Nicklaus after a weak round of golf went to the practice range immediately after playing the 18th hole. He worked until dark with little hope of finding solution. While asleep that night, the solution came as a dream. His golf round the next day was a brilliant display of execution. This was not an isolated incidence as he experienced it several times. Not only Nicklaus but also other golfers and athletes have had similar revelations. Since Brehtt was an ex-athlete, he followed this procedure and has had success with it. This experience seems to verify the old wives' tale or myth of "I'll sleep on it" when someone needs more analytical time on a project.

He wakes up, dresses, goes down to the lobby of his apartment building and gets the newspaper. Returns to his apartment and opens the paper, glances at the first page and notices the picture of a prominent local citizen who died unexpectedly from a heart attack. This he reads thoroughly. He then proceeds to the obituary columns for more details on the person, death, family, funeral home, burial, etc.

The man, Dr. Joseph P. Smith was a nationally prominent physician.

"He has money."

He was an avid golfer, and an ex-minor league baseball player. His wife was about his age, 35, and from the photo of her in the paper looks good, very good.

"I like her, real sexy."

Brehtt's brain is now flying at full speed. He has to slow down so that he does not go past or forget a strategic plan. Out comes his note pad to write down the details of funeral home, times, full family names, etc.

Perfect execution of his plan is essential. One little slip up like messing up a name may reveal his con. His plan will be checked repeatedly so that everything will be automatic and natural.

Godly Heavens Funeral Home

Brehtt walks in with his funeral face. Looks around, mingles in the crowd and in time moves to the widow. When no one is around her, he moves in and offers his condolences.

"I do not know you, or should I?" the bereaved wife utters.

"We do not know each other, but Joe and I played many rounds of golf together with a few card games thrown in. I enjoyed his company and I will miss him greatly. Our games were highly competitive, friendly and fun."

Mrs. Smith's face loses its mourning look to a face of sternness. "Ah, does he owe you money. I did not approve of his gambling. I just accepted it as part of him. How much does he owe you?"

"This is not the time, nor am I here to collect. I am here out of respect to him and your loss. The bets are off the table, so forget them."

Her face changes to one of compassion. A smile creeps up into her face. To change the subject, Brehtt asks, "Do you play golf?"

"Yes, I do, in fact, excuse my vanity but I am the women's club champion at the Lions Gate Country Club, but I do not gamble at golf nor am I interested in card games. Cards are so boring."

"You sound like an adventurous woman," as he knows women like to be considered adventurous but will not usually admit it. "Perhaps when things settle down we might play a round of golf with no betting and no card games after the round."

"That would be nice and it would be nice to meet my husband's mysterious friend. Give me a month for things to settle," as she extends her hand which Brehtt shakes.

He mingles around with casual talk here and there to get the feel of his friends. After all, he never knew the man, the wife or family so he must pick up little hints and clues from the friends. He sticks around until the burial time and then proceeds in the procession to the cemetery. He is one of the last to leave as this shows great respect. He then gives his hand to the widow with a short condolence and leaves happy as hell, as things are falling into place as planned.

One Month Later
"Hello."
"Mrs. Smith, this is Brehtt Bennett. How is everything going? Are you adjusting well?"

"Brehtt. How nice of you to call. I am adjusting well and ready for a round of golf. I have not played lately and I would really enjoy a game. And Brehtt, please call me Brenda."

"Well, I am free anytime so why don't you arrange a tee time that fits into your schedule and phone me back." He closes his phone and ponders.

"Good timing. Adjusting to a new lifestyle as a widow can be tough. Right now, she is at her most lonely stage. Wait too long and a widow adjusts to the single life."

An hour later Brenda phones Brehtt. "Brehtt, this is Brenda. We have a tee time at 1:35 on this coming Tuesday at Lions Gate Country Club. I took the 1:35 tee time so that we can eat dinner at the club after the round. OK."

"Sounds great. See you Tuesday. Bye."

"Take this one slow. Get her confidence first then casually mention the deal but brush it off and then let it play on her mind. Then when she is ready, move in for the kill."

Brehtt arrives early and finds Brenda on the practice range. "Hey, this is not fair. No one practices before a friendly round. I do like your swing. Boy, I think I may be in trouble, so I will not play you for money."

Brenda smiles and almost blushes. "Let's get some bottled water before we tee off."

They make it to the tee box and tee off. Since the lady's tee boxes are in front of the men's, Brehtt tee off first, and then takes the cart to the lady's tee box.

Brehtt is a golf hustler. He knows never to play a good shot unless it is necessary. Never show the con what you got. With this, he hits a looping slice out to the left but comes back to the fairway. Brenda hit the usual club champion's drive. Down the middle and long by women's standards.

"Nice drive. Are you good or lucky?

"Both."

"Yeah, it's true isn't it sometimes in this game you have to be a little lucky?"

The game continues with a few barbs and trash talks, all in fun. Brenda completely enjoys herself. She enjoys giving and receiving the barbs and trash talk.

At the end of the round Brenda says, "Brehtt, I enjoyed this round of golf so much. This is the most fun I've had since . . . since . .."

Brehtt cuts her off, "I know. I understand." He moves in and gives her a reassuring hug. She enjoys the short moment of intimacy which has been absent since the funeral. They proceed into the clubhouse for dinner.

The dinner goes well. They talk, they laugh, and they tease. They leave for the parking lot and to their cars. Brehtt walks her to her car, she clicks the remote, the door unlocks, and Brehtt opens the door. Brenda turns to back into the seat and now faces Brehtt. "Thank you so much. It was a day I needed so badly to get out of my doldrums. If you do not mind, and you can work it in, can we do this again sometime? I would be so grateful."

"Definitely, it was too enjoyable not to do it again. Since it is your golf club make it for next Friday and phone me."

"Wonderful," She responds. "Bye for now. Oh, and bring your 'A' game. You looked a little rusty out there. I am not your once a month housewife golfer. I know hidden talent even when it does not all come out." She then leans forward and kisses Brehtt on the cheek. I nice kiss and a little longer than necessary for a cheek kiss.

"You cheeky bastard," a trashy claim by Brehtt.

They laugh. She drives off and he walks to his car.

"My God, this is going faster than I thought. Was that kiss a message? A couple of more dates and the game can be solidified. She will be ready."

For the next three weeks, they date at dinners, movies, golf, shopping, etc. On the fourth week, they return to her place after dinner and a movie. They enter her apartment and proceed to the sofa. They sit down, each acting nonchantly but each knowing what could happen next. They both look around as if to make sure they are alone. Then like too magnets they face each other with no elements of doubt in knowing what they want – they kiss. A long, wet, sloppy, hungry kiss that lasts and lasts. Hands move into position on each other. Forty-five minutes later she freezes. "Brehtt, I am so sorry, I am not ready for the full commitment. I am just not ready. It was nice and I enjoyed it. I am sorry if I mislead you."

"I enjoyed it also. I will leave now. I understand."

THE DEAL

On the fifth hole of the country club, Brehtt asks, "You know, did Joe ever talk to you about his interest in the wasted area on 33rd street?"

"No."

"Ok. Never mind then."

"The seed is planted. By not telling, her curiosity is building."

"Tell me."

"Her curiosity is peeking."

"Oh, it is not very interesting. You know how us men like to talk and bullshit. It was really nothing."

"You tell me or get the fuck off this golf course immediately."

"Well, that empty lot is just a waste. We used to watch the kids play games, baseball, soccer, basketball, and a kiddy area with swing, teeter totters, etc. on an old field with cement area that were once flooring, junk and garbage. A real mess. He said that he would like to make it a park for the kids in the area, keep'em off the streets and getting into trouble. Those kids hang around with time on their hands with nothing to do. That is not good. Joe said he had the money and would like to build a park and call it the Joseph P. Smith Youth Park. Anyway that was the idea but he is gone now so let's just forget it."

"Like hell you will forget it. I love it. Let's get started." She is charged up and slams her drive down the fairway. We eat and discuss it further after this round."

Off they go to inspect the wasteland. They then go to city hall for the details on the land. Back taxes are high about $210,000. The clerk says that they may give a 10 percent discount but that is all. The tax is high so no one wants to take it.

"But, that . . ."

"Thank you for your help," as he grabs Benda by the arm and leads her out.

"Don't say anything. I know the mayor. I can work this out. Just do not let on anything to anybody about this deal. In two days, you will be happy as hell.

ONE DAY LATER
Brehtt meets with the mayor.
"Jim, we see each other on the golf course so let's get to the point. That waste area on 33rd street is just a waste and eye sore. I have a client who is willing to buy the land and fix it up as a youth park for baseball, soccer, basketball, and a kiddy area with swings, etc. they want $210,000 in back taxes. What say you delete the back taxes and give us the land?"

"Brehtt, I can't do that. That is a lot of money."

"Ok, you owe me $35,000 in lost bets with me in golf. You are not doing a good job in paying back so I will drop your payments to me if you give us the land."

"Ok, I can work a deal. How 'bout if I give the land to your client for $100,000."

"Shit, here comes my heavy artillery."

"Jim, the land is for a park for the kids, remember Jim, I said for the kids. Projects by the city for the kids means a lot to the parents, and parents you dumb shit, means votes. Am I making myself clear? You don't give us the land word goes out that you nixed the park and you lose votes in the coming election in four months. All you have to do is delete the tax, building the park starts immediately, parents and kids are happy, you get votes and you do not have to pay back your golf debts."

"Ok, asshole, you win. Pick up your deed tomorrow afternoon. Remember, no one knows about this conversation."

"Of course not," they shake hands and both are pleased with the proverbial win/win silliness.

TWO DAYS LATER
Brehtt has picked up the deed and goes to Benda's house. He shows her the deed. Brenda, "This is between you and me. Do not ask questions. The deed cost us $50,000. You give me the $50,000 and we talk to the construction people tomorrow.

Brenda is so happy; she grabs Brehtt and gives him a big passionate kiss.

Brehtt gets the construction crew set up. They go over plans and needs. The construction cost will be $115,000, but Brehtt plans on using volunteer help by the parents to lower costs. Brehtt knows the construction owner and the deal is a quiet deal with all transactions between the owner and Brehtt. Brenda Smith does not know the expenses. All she knows is that it will cost $115,000. She has the money so what the hell.

> "I can make a least 30 thousand on this and still give the construction owner a 10 thousand bonus. Brenda is happy with the project and she will have no input so it should be a safe deal."

The park is built. Brehtt made $50,000 thousand on the deed deal and $30 thousand on the construction and the construction owner made $10,000 bonus.

And, despite all the under the table deals, Brenda is happy as hell. There is a big sign, seen for miles:

THE DR. JOSEPH P. SMITH
MEMORIAL YOUTH PARK

To Brenda, money cannot buy this sign and the park. It is everything.

CHAPTER 4

THE SPY LADY

The next day, Natasha is sitting at the café's window hoping Stella will drop in for lunch. No luck. This was repeated several times but no lunch. Finally, the next Monday, Stella walked into the café, turned left and stopped while starring into the eyes of Natasha. They smiled at each other; Natasha stood and said, "Please sit down with me. A little conversation would be nice." Stella wandered over and sat kind of studying Natasha with a not knowing why.

"I'm so glad for a chance to apologize again. I feel bad about my haste and coffee stains on your dress."

"Dry cleaning did not work. Did you ever notice the more expensive the material the more fragile it is."

"Natasha giggles and agrees.

"Your generosity means that I will buy another."

"Were do you do that?"

"I go to Chez Femme, it is convenient and it is just a few stores down the sidewalk."

"I've never been there. If you do not mind, can I go with you and also look around?"

"Uhh . . . errr. . . ok."

Natasha pays the bill and out the door they go, two women doing what women do – shop.

They look around and evaluate different styles and models. Each in turn pulling one off the rack, holding up, "This is gorgeous. It would look good on you."

"You think so?" is the reply to this and all the other dresses.

Shopping, evaluating and analyzing all the goods takes time but finally they pick one for Stella. Stella loves it and encourages Natasha to also get one. Natasha picks one kind of along the same lines but in different color and with enough of a difference because two women cannot wear the same dress. The dress was similar enough to show a similarity of personality which helps bond her to Stella, and yet different enough to not be the same. Natasha recalls, in her high style lifestyle parties of women ready to fight when they appear in a luxurious, expensive dress to find someone also at the party wearing an identical dress. Hostility.

They pay and walk out. "This is so much fun, shopping with someone whose tastes are similar to mine. This is new to me," an excited Stella tells Natasha.

Natasha's eyes light up. "Hey, let's go to Victoria's Secret and Fredericks and finish the job," as she waves her arm for a taxi.

"Oh, no. I could never do that. I would be embarrassed and uncomfortable. I have never done anything like that. Besides I am not really that good looking or sexy."

"Honey, you just do not know how beautiful and sexy you are. I've been around and you are on the top of the list," Natasha responds while gently caressing Stella's shoulder.

The taxi pulls up. Natasha opens the door. Stella hesitates. "Come pretty girl. Let's look at the wild side. Natasha gently leads the reluctant lady into the taxi. She watches Stella slide into the taxi as her skirt rides up above her knees, well above her knees. She almost sees it. The camel toe, the vagina, the pussy, or whatever you want to call it. . . a rose by any other name is still a rose. Despite her excitement, Natasha still realizes this must be a slow seduction, a strong seduction so that in time she can her trust and then her husband's information. She also realizes her drive to dominate Stella is a feeling spreading through her body. Stella is captivating Natasha's psyche. Stella is most beautiful. Stella will become a submissive toy.

Off they go and Stella is still blushing as they go into Victoria's Secret. The bras, panties, crotchless panties, even corsets, bras with open nipple space, mini dresses, low V-neck blouses, etc., etc.

"Oh, my, oh I have never seen anything like this," blushes Stella.

"Neat, eh," replies Natasha.

"Stella, look at this. This bra is yours. The color, lace, etc. matches your skin tone, hair color and new dress."

"To the dressing room, this is you and the new dress," as she almost drags Stella to the dressing room. They both go in and shut the door. Natasha has to help Stella off with her blouse and bra. Stella is nude from the waist up. Natasha is staring at the perfect breasts just inches from her lips. She lifts the bra, leans over to Stella; they are almost touching breast to breast. She pulls the bra up to the nipples, places it over each breast, and then reaches around to fasten it at her back. Natasha feels good that it is not with a clasp on the front. As she fastens it, she slowly breathes into the ear of Stella who thinks it is just an accident. Stella stiffens and then relaxes, enjoying the moment. Natasha knows she is winning the battle.

Stella looks in the mirror. Smiles and realizes it looks good. With a weak voice she says, "I like it. We will get it. It is so nasty."

Natasha realizes she said, "We'll get it" and not "I'll get it." A bonding and familiarity is building between them with the word we. Natasha realizes seduction is moving faster than believed. This woman is longing for love but her feelings were inhibited. Her protective shell is breaking.

"This we will buy but we need more stuff. Let me release the clasp so we can shop more," softly says Natasha. She reaches around Stella to undo the clasp behind her. In so doing, she leans against her nude upper body. She breathes in her ear again as she undoes the clasp and letting the bra fall from the breasts. Stella does not stiffen of move, her eyes are closed and she is blushing.

In a daring move, Natasha drops her head, kisses her left nipple, and gives it a quick lick. Stella moves her breast forward and not away. She is delighted with the kiss, the lick and naturally wants more. Her arms encircle Natasha's head pulling her close. Stella is thinking how long it has been without sex and physical love. She realizes it now as she begs, "Don't stop. I love it." It is so good she is not even concerned that it is a woman, lesbian sex that has taken over her heterosexual past. Soon, Stella dresses and they walk out for more shopping.

The seed has been planted and Stella's sex life is now raging out of control, much to the delight of Natasha. They bought the store out. If it was sexy, they bought it. Arms full of bags they walk out of the store to the street and hail a taxi.

"Let's go to my place and try all these on," asks Natasha.

"Yeahhh," comes the reply.

THE CON MAN

Brehtt lies down and reminiscences a little of the past venture and what is next. He picks up a book and reads. The material in this book is research on how to influence people. It also covers some interesting cons, which is right up his alley. Brehtt is no flimflam con guy. He studies the science behind the con so that he does not fall victim to a silly mistake or careless error that will destroy the fraud and land him in jail.

When he imitates an expert in the area of his scam, he knows that experts carry considerable knowledge in the area of the scam. Therefore, to play the expert he does his research. The library and internet are a vast source on information for him. Biographies of con artists are also helpful. He leaves nothing to chance. However, this knowledge is often not enough. The knowledge is based on how well he can convey the knowledge with confidence to be completely believable. It is not only the message, but also how the message is conveyed.

In the book, one of the chapters is on reciprocation, a potent weapon to the con artist. This means when someone does something for us we reciprocate with a similar action. A neighbor cuts your lawn, and will not charge, we reciprocate with an action like bringing a pie over the next day. If someone buys us lunch, we reciprocate by paying for his lunch the next day. The con artist wants to be the first to make the favor so that the target is then compelled to return the favor, and often the favor is returned. So simple, and yet so effective.

Christmas is a time for lots of reciprocation. Christmas cards are exchanged every year because someone sends you a card so you send them a card. If someone forgets to send a card then no card is sent to that person the next year. In fact, this procedure often has people keeping a list of received cards so only they get a card the next year.

What about gifts? Gifts are exchanged, and if someone sends a gift of lesser value, then next year that person will get a gift of lesser value. As we see, reciprocation is a balancing act of value for value.

The con artists uses this by a favor, gift or benefit to his target, knowing that somewhere down the line he will get it back.

> *"Interesting, mulls Brehtt in thought, and how he used it with Jim Sullivan, the mayor, to get the land for the youth park free. Brehtt cancelled the golf debt Jim had with him so Jim had to reciprocate with the free land. He had to force a little with reasoning but he still got the reciprocation he wanted from his target."*

Reciprocation is big in politics. If you vote for my bill, I will vote for your bill when it comes up. This is not good because sometimes the person may not like the bill as it can be detrimental, but he has to vote for the bill to reciprocate the guy who voted for his bill.

Political rallies give free food and boring speeches hoping that the people will reciprocate with their votes.

In love and sex, reciprocation is evident. A dinner and movies date is often a move for reciprocation by the woman to have sex. After marriage the flowers, movies, dinner, etc. fade away and the woman's sexual favors fade away.

Some stores will offer free hot dogs and soda so the clientele will reciprocate by spending more money. Grocery stores often do this.

Reciprocation must be known, understood and applied for the con.

CHAPTER 5

THE SPY LADY

They unload the packages, look at them and then strip to try them on again. They laugh, giggle and have fun but they do not get into too many items. Stella is now inhibition free and moves to help Natasha with her shoulder straps on the dress. Her hands touch Natasha with electric feelings. Natasha moans, reaches out and pulls her closer. They kiss. Long, wet and sloppy. The way lovers should kiss. The dress never makes it on the body but is on the floor with panties and bra on top of the dress. Soon no clothes. Two nude bodies are pressed.

Three hours later, Stella says she must get home. Ralph, her husband is leaving the country in the morning so she feels it is best to be home tonight and help him pack.

"Where is he going?"

"Top secret. Going to Syria says the media, but I saw his itinery and he is going to the Ukraine to spy on Russian movements. I saw it when he went into the bathroom and I glanced. It is secret because they do not want the Russians to know the CIA is aware of Russia's possible aid for the rebels. It is covert.

"When he is gone can we visit?" Natasha coos.

"Of course, I will be offended if we do not," Stella replies.

Stella pulls out her business card, writes her private cell number on the card, and gives it to Natasha. Natasha also exchanges her card.

THE CON MAN

BACK ON TRACK

Brehtt mopes around for an hour and then decides to go out to eat and have a few beers. He goes to the restaurant and looks around for a seat, as it is crowded. As he walks down the aisle, he sees a young lady eating alone. As he passes, he looks at her and smiles. She smiles back, but he keeps on walking past a few more tables, turns back around and proceeds to the young lady again.

"I hope you don't mind, but it is crowded in here and I am wondering if you would mind if I sat at your table. You don't have to talk to me, but it would be nice not having to eat alone."

> *"I'm playing on her sympathy of helping out a stranger. After all, it is perfectly safe with this stranger."*

"I understand so well. Have a seat. I will enjoy the company and I will even talk to you." This gives both a laugh. The ice breaker works.

Brehtt learns that she is a college student doing graduate work in sociology and social work.

> *"Ahh, maybe she is a "help the people person. Isn't that what social work is?"*

They talk like old friends and he eventually finds out that college students are always in need of money.

> *"Maybe, we can try something to get her some money for her college debts. Looking deep into her eyes, he outlines a plan that she hesitantly accepts but soon is keen as hell."*

They leave the restaurant and proceed down the street to a popular bar catering to older clientele. She walks in alone, sits down at the bar and has a drink. 40 minutes later, she goes to the toilet and then returns to the bar, sits down and finishes her drink. As she rises from her stool, she scratches her neck and notices her necklace is gone. In panic mode, she returns to the bar and asks the bartender if anyone turned in a necklace. The bartender says no and she then starts to cry. She cries loud and receives all the attention.

"The necklace is an expensive heirloom, handed down by many family generations. My father will kill me if it is not found. I know he will offer a reward of at least 5,000 dollars. I am so scared. I must get it back. If someone finds it, I will let him fuck me all night as another reward. On wobbly legs she gets a pen from the bartender and gives him her address and phone number. Still crying she goes out the door and says that her name is Emily James and I am at the Holiday Inn for tonight and tomorrow only.

The men start looking around and Brehtt walks in while everyone is searching. He sits at the bar, orders his drink and proceeds to the toilet. He comes out with a necklace in his hand and asks the bartender who owns the necklace he found in the men's toilet. "I guess some woman was so drunk she went into the wrong toilet."

The men look at him with envy.

Well, I guess I will take it home and give it to my wife," utters Brehtt. "It's no good to me," as he slips the necklace into his pocket.

The bartender then says that he will take it and see that it is returned. Brehtt looks at him and says, "I used to work in a bar and I know those things are never returned."

"I will give you 100 dollars for the necklace."

"Why."

"For my wife."

Someone then yells he will give 250 for the necklace.

Brehtt perks up. "Why?" He pulls the necklace out of his pocket and says, "It does look expensive." Brehtt is now an auctioneer as the bidding goes up to over 1,000 dollars.

"Is it the money or the all night fucking that has the men so worked up?"

Finally, from the back a well-dressed man rises from his seat, walks over to Brehtt and puts 2,000 down in front of him.

"Good enough," says Brehtt and gives him the necklace. Brehtt is out the door to his car with Emily driving. He jumps into the already open door and off they speed.

Later, they stop and Brehtt gives her the split of 1,000. She jumps over and gives him a big, long kiss.

CHAPTER 6

THE SPY LADY

The next day, Natasha fills out her assignment result forms. She places them in a briefcase and phones using her code and pay as you go cell phone to inform of the drop.

The drop takes place at her nearby Dairy Queen. She goes in and sits down with the briefcase on the floor near her feet but well away from nearby patrons. She nibbles on her sundae while looking for her contact. Once she sees him, she leaves her half-eaten sundae and briefcase and walks to the lady's room so that any patrons seeing the sundae and briefcase will think she is just going for a tinkle. The timing is perfect. As she leaves the lady's room, the contact sits near her table. Looks around, reaches for the briefcase and while rushing to the exit yells in a loud voice, "You left your briefcase." He runs out the door just as Natasha's Lamborghini is driving away. No one suspects anything and so the exchange is made and the Russians have their information.

On waking up the next day there is a pale blue envelop on the floor slipped under the door. She opens it and reads, *"Good job. This was quicker than we thought. We now know more about the CIA envoy and their true objectives. Now we can take counter measures to hide our ultimate objective. Keep contact with Stella for more information. Wonderful work."*

THE CON MAN
REMINISCENCE
In the middle of the night, Brehtt wakes up, shakes his head and rubs his eyes. His mind slowly thinks of his past scams. He likes to do this so that he can evaluate his past performances for improvement. All scams must be constantly evaluated for perfect execution next time.

Brehtt rehearses in his mind the three rules for a scam: plan, perform and then evaluate.

"THE PLAN. Everything must be planned. Is the environment right? Is the money there and is the risk worth the reward? What is the escape route if needed? Is alcohol consumption a risk, a hindrance or is it needed to build the trust? All such things are planned by running a movie in my mind. As the movie runs, stops are made for possible adverse outcomes, like what may happen if this happens. Murphy's Law is a major component in planning. The way to counteract "If something can go wrong, it will" is to be prepared for it. Be ready with the alibi and not be caught in a surprise moment. Showing confidence in the adverse moments often deletes any skepticism."

"PERFORMANCE. Execution must be perfect. Failure of execution may not only mean loss of the scam and money but the possibility of physical abuse or damage to my body by irate marks or targets. The danger here is mob mentality. If the target suspects a con job, the target may follow with punching, hitting and kicking. Sometimes this can result in death or near death experience. This means performance must be practiced, just like a highly skilled athlete, practice, practice and more practice until perfect."

"EVALUATION. This may be the most important of all, but in no way making the other two less important. This is where corrections are made for future scams. Reevaluating the marks, the situation, Murphy's Law, everything. Every little detail. Evaluation make cons better the next time. Evaluation must not miss anything."

"And I must not forget the three rules of create the hook, line and sinker. The old adage of the con man."

Brehtt picks up his research book and reads:

THE HOOK is getting the mark or marks interested. In most cases, it works best when the mark comes to you. When the mark comes to you he has shown his interest, he is hooked. If you chase the mark you may have to fast talk, glib talk to get him interested and it may be a waste of time.

Getting the mark interested is a subtle approach. The trick or scam can be done with a friend as an aide. I show the trick to the friend usually in a bar, but fail to accomplish or succeed in doing the trick. After a few tries someone will usually come over and ask what I'm trying to do. Sometimes the trick is tried alone and someone will come over to watch and inquire. Either way you may have the mark. Talk is exchanged to give time for more marks to come over where the con leads the discussion to bets. Alcohol often gives the mark a feeling of bravery, confidence and intelligence, of which are usually false or overblown. Now if the con has a pretty woman with him the bets increase, not only for the false bravery, confidence and intelligence but also in the attempt to impress a pretty woman. To the con, alcohol and a pretty woman are great assets.

THE LINE is the talk - persuasive, glib, fluent, smooth and convincing to the marks to move the bets up. The line may take a few minutes to increase the anticipation of the marks. They want their money immediately. Often, the con will feign interest in the bets as he even shows doubts that the trick can be done. When the time is ripe and the money is on the table, the scam is executed. The mark and his girlfriend pick up the money and exit quickly.

Some of the best cons are women, although we hear very little of them. Good-looking women have the best hook and line in their body and brain. A good-looking woman can lead a man so easily. The man thinks he is impressing the woman with his macho attitude and his bravado and his belief, usually false, in being the great lover, the stud that this woman needs. This is his downfall as the woman now has the rope to lead him into the con. Women have done some of the biggest cons in having men steal, extort, and even kill for them.

THE SINK is when the marks have been conned. The mark has sunk into depravity and embarrassment. The mark sinks when he thinks with the wrong head. When the penis head and the brain head are in conflict, the penis wins the struggle to leave the man beaten.

Brehtt's reminiscence fades away and he falls back into sleep as the book falls to the floor. He wakes up, has breakfast and watches the TV news as he eats.

He stops with his mouth gaping open at the TV and the announcer tells of the big Shriners convention in town. He listens for the particulars, the time, date, theme, etc. He gets up and phones Emily James, the graduate student social worker, who also majors in the theatre. She is good looking. He used her before. She can act and she has 'balls'. Is this not ideal?

CHAPTER 7

THE SPY LADY

7:30 am her phone rings. She rolls trying to reach it on the nightstand. Her eyes cannot see. 7:30 am. Nobody wakes this early. Groggily, a hello is uttered. On the other end is a cheerfull, "Hi. I was thinking of you so I called to see if you would like to do something today. I'm taking the day off," says a cheerful Stella.

"OK. Why don't you come over and help me get ready. You sound up and ready."

"Be right over."

True enough, she is right over and knocking on the door. Natasha opens the door and Stella falls right into Natasha's arms, hugging and kissing. Looks like they will not make it out to do something. After several hours of play, Natasha drifts the talk to Ralph. Stella talks honestly about their relationship and admits to Natasha how much she is enjoying their relationship despite her marriage. Stella reveals much about her husband but little about his involvement in government affairs as it is mostly top secret. She did reveal that the USA was building and planning to increase involvement in a covert way for Ukraine rebels. Stella knows she should not be saying anything but she feels it is minor information and just lover's secrets.

Natasha feels she is making headway but will not push for information. The day continues with conversation, sex, conversation, sex, conversation and eating. Natasha reveals in her conversation that she is recently divorced from a rich businessman with an extremely good settlement so she does not have to work. Just enjoy life. Money is no problem.

"You are so lucky. You are so happy. You are so sexual."

"Well, you are sexual too. Really," says Natasha as a confidence builder for Stella.

"No, I am very inhibited and scared to let go. I want to be like you, as long as my husband does not find out."

Natasha strides one-step forward while Stella copies the move. No words. Stella is shaking in anticipation. She is getting excited. Her eyelids droop and then close as Natasha's lips lock onto hers. They cling tightly and Natasha says, "Come with me to my lair. We are going to discuss and experiment on your awakening, your sexual awakening."

Natasha's mind is reeling. *"Once she goes wild, as she is ready, a little loving blackmail will get more information on her husband's activities and governmental manoeuvers. This is going to be easy and yet so much fun."*

As they lie on the king-size waterbed, gasping for breath, Natasha asks Stella, "How would you like to go wild. Your husband is gone for a month, everything we do will be discreet, no one will know, and if they do, nothing will be said.

"I have a club. A very special club where only certain people can be members. The members are wealthy and prominent in society. It is a social sex club but some members go, sex or no sex. They just attend for the social atmosphere. The sex is there when wanted and no one is forced or coerced into anything. The word no means no. All forms of sex are available."

"Oh, it sounds wonderful, but I would not know how to act. I would want to but I would be scared of messing up."

"Here's what we do. We go and just observe. No requirements or expectations. We just get a feel for the place. I can arrange for this

Saturday. You can wear your new sexy attire we purchased the other day.

"Ok, but just a look see," Stella nervously responds.

Natasha rolls over onto Stella, "I love you so much. We are going to have a blast."

THE CON MAN

THE SHRINER'S CONVENTION

Emily and Brehtt enter the Holiday Inn and move to the second floor for the convention. On the way to the second floor, Brehtt gives Emily a wedding ring to wear as wives are invited to these functions. They proceed to the main greeting table with all the nametags displayed. Emily shifts away from Brehtt to draw the greeter's eyesight away from Brehtt who is now able to grab a nametag and slip it into his pocket. He then excuses himself from Emily with the toilet excuse and quickly goes to his car, opens his laptop and prints out on the portable printer his name in the same font as the legitimate tags. He could have used the nametag he stole from the table, but that is a little risky as someone may notice the name is different from the body. He rushes back in, apologizes to Emily for his delay. With the nametag in place, they enter the large room with tables, gaming tables, a few slot machines, a blackjack table and a craps table. They get a couple of drinks, coffee, and sit at a table where they talk, laugh and act like they are having a good time.

When Brehtt finishes his coffee, he notices that some of the people have moved near their table. He looks at Emily. The game is on.

Emily giggles and then says loud enough for the people nearby hear, "No, no," then a giggle and "It's not that long." She laughs again, "You men have no eyesight for measurement." The men turn around captivated by their interpretations of her comments. Emily gives the men her come on glance. The men smile and not realizing it, they are hooked.

One of them asked if they could get in on this conversation, as it sounds interesting.

"Ok," says Emily. "He wants to know if the circumference of the mug is longer than the height of the mug. I told him he was stupid as the circumference is longer."

Emily is leading them on.

Brehtt then enters with, "So if the circumference is longer, then what if I put a deck of cards and a pack of cigarettes under the coffee mug. Which is longer."

"They are about the same."

"Are you guys sure? How sure?"

"Here's ten dollars."

"Not very sure are you? Ok, if I put another deck of cards under the mug are you convinced as to your bet being correct in that the height from table top to brim is longer than the circumference?"

"Yes."

"If you are right I will give you each 100 dollars. If I am right, each of you will give me 100 dollars.

"Fair enough."

"Money on the table please. $1,100 from the 11 men is on the table with Brehtt's 1,100.

Brehtt takes a string from his pocket, measures the circumference, and then shows that the height measurement is still shorter than the circumference.

The men have been stung. They stand there gaping in disbelief. Emily and Brehtt pick up the money, thank the gentlemen, and exit quickly.

They drive away and then decide to have a drink at a popular bar. It is getting late into the evening and most customers will be well lubed and perhaps just short of drunk.

They enter and proceed immediately to the bar. Emily finds a table, centrally located to the customers. Brehtt brings two martinis and sits down. The place is jumping with people wandering all over.

In time, Brehtt finishes his drink and places his drinking coaster over the martini glass. To get the attention of the crowd he asks around for a cigarette. Naturally, he is told he cannot smoke in here but he explains that he is trying an experiment to show his girlfriend. "Yeah, I'm trying to impress her." They both laugh.

"Can I watch the experiment?"

"Sure, even your friends can watch. We like company."

Brehtt and the new friend walk over to the table to Emily. He takes the cigarette, balances it on the coaster on top of the martini glass, and places a quarter on the end of the cigarette.

"Now Emily, can you get the quarter into the martini glass without touching any of the props, banging the table, etc."

"Hey guys, come here, this is neat," yells the new friend.

The hook is in.

Brehtt now delivers the line. "I bet her one dollar she cannot do it, but I can."

"No, it cannot be done. I will bet 20 dollars you can't."

"It is very tricky and I have done it two out of five times so the odds are in your favor. But I feel confident tonight."

"Maybe, but not this time."

Several people are now crowded around the table.

"I will match the money you put on the table." This gets them going. Tens, twenties, and fifties are bet. The total is 950 dollars."

Brehtt gets off his chair, does a little stretch, rubs his hands for dexterity, goes to his knees on the floor, and blows sharply upwards on the underside of the beer coaster. The coaster flips upwards and away from the martini glass, the cigarette flies away and the quarter, hangs and then drops into the glass.

A thank you is expressed. Emily has the money. They exit the bar, into their car and drive away.

CHAPTER 8

THE SPY LADY

Natasha on the phone, "Stella, why don't you come to my place after work and stay here until our Saturday night party."

Stella does. And, what do they do? Well, sex was the main issue, but Natasha also uses the time to indoctrinate Stella into the passions of an orgy. Dildo, vibrators, and strap-on penises were played with to bring familiarity to the upcoming orgy. Oral sex techniques for men and women from the Kama Sutra were practiced.

Natasha explained the Kama Sutra to an avid Stella who is all ears. "The Kama Sutra is an ancient Hindu book that is often considered the standard in human sexuality. It describes positions, pleasures, and techniques for the best sex possible. The word Kama is a goal of Hindu life in a desire for life and a desire for sexuality. Sutra literally means the line that hold all life together. The Kama Sutra is not just a sex manual it is a guide to life, nature, love, family and all pleasures of life and happiness. Yes, sex is part of life, a strong part. We are going to enjoy these pleasures of life."

"Yes, yes, oh my yes. I have left myself so sheltered. I have missed so much of life. I have so much to make up. My life has been full of inhibitions and limits, with little or no pleasure. I WANT PLEASURE," she screams. Grabs Natasha and hugs her passionately.

They spend the evening talking and playing. They talk about their families and home life of the late and early years. Natasha reveals her twin brother who she rarely sees. "He doesn't really like me. He is conservative and I am a slut, whore, degenerate according to him. When we do see each other, we talk little. Fortunately we are both well off.

Natasha's mind is whirling, "*God, I hope I do not have to blackmail her for information on her husband. She is so much fun now that she has opened up. I could fall in love with her but I can't. . . oh, shit maybe I can get her onto my side and work together. She is almost at the point of doing whatever I ask of her. Ahh, love can be so manipulative.*"

THE CON MAN

REMINISCENCE

Brehtt lying in bed reading the biography of Alvin Clarence Thomas alias "Titanic Thompson". His head drops and the book slides out of his hands, down his body and onto the floor. He dreams:

Titanic may well be the most famous con man of all time. This is why he is Brehtt's hero. His cons were magnificent and well planned. Often his cons were set up in advance like the time he took a big spender for 1,000 dollars as they came out of a building.

Titanic bet the guy that the next car to come around the corner would have a license plate with three threes. Looking like a good bet the guy takes it. In a few minutes, a taxi comes round the corner. Titanic waved him down. They check the license plate and to the surprise of the guy – three threes. Titanic takes the money, jumps into the cab and drives away. When out of range, Titanic pays the cabby $100 for following his plan.

Alvin got the name Titanic because he was supposed to have been on the Titanic when it sank. A lifeboat saved him and took him to safety. Is the story true or is it folklore? No one knows the real answer but true or false stories like this always go with con men.

Brehtt, like Titanic, is highly skilled in various activities, especially golf. Titanic would do the old hustle scam. Move into a town and search around for a big money game. In golf, these games are readily available because most golfers think their game is better than it actually. The inflated ego is what the con man thrives on. The old myth, I would like to buy him for what he is worth and sell him for what he thinks he is worth is so true. On getting a game, arrangements are made, especially in the rules, which are close to the USGA official rules, but may have a few deviations.

During the game, Titanic shoots 85 while the opponent shoots 73. Titanic loses badly so after the game Titanic asks for a rematch. His excuse being unfamiliarity with the course. The opponent and the friends who bet on the match giggle some and say that they will give a rematch but he is really out of his league.

Titanic feigns anger. "I can beat you anytime I want to. In fact, I will play left handed, unlike today when I played right handed, except we triple the stakes to 10,000 dollars." The guys are wowed – easy money. The game is on tomorrow at 1:30.

At 1:30 pm the opponent and the fans are there, but no Titanic. Titanic is waiting in a coffee shop eating and drinking in a leisurely style. At 2:00 he leaves and goes to the golf course a mile away.

The golf course fans are agitated but not as much as the opponent. He is on edge waiting. At 2:10 pm Titanic pulls into the parking lot without a care in the world, takes his time getting ready and proceeds to the first tee. Comments and heckles proceed, "Hurry up." "You're late." "You're scared?" are comments from the gallery.

Titanic is unfazed. He tees up and rips one down the middle, picks up his tee, looks at his opponent, smiles and gets out of the way for him to hit.

The opponent, with a little anger, naturally swings too fast, a little quick, well, maybe a lot quick. The ball is hit a long way but into the water hazard on the left.

The first hole is an indication of the round. The opponent settles down on the back nine and shoots a 74. Titanic cruises in with a 68.

Titanic shakes hands, collects his money and drives off with 10,000 dollars in his pocket. Titanic is the only one who knows that he is a natural left hand golfer.

He drives on his way to the next sucker."

Brehtt continues his sleep with a mile wide grin.

CHAPTER 9

THE SPY LADY

Friday night passes by into Saturday. They are worn out. Stella has learned so much. Her soul is free. They sleep solidly till almost noon. They slowly rise and shuffle to breakfast of waffles smothered in strawberries and whipped cream. White grape juice finishes the meal. They look at each other, smile and run back to bed.

6:15 pm they are up, showering, make-upping with the rouge, lipstick, mascara, aloe cream, and hair spray. From sleepy eyes a few hours ago they eyes are now sparkling, alert and excited. Their heartbeats pick up a little. They move to their dresses, trying each on only to reject and try another while waiting for approval from the other. Finally, they make it. Short miniskirts, four-inch heels, blouses and shirts with belly buttons revealed and lots of cleavage accentuated with their frilly and lacy push-up bras. They are ready.

Out the door and down the hall to the elevators, but they do not go to the park-in garage.

"We go by taxi and not Lamborghini. We will be in no shape to drive the next morning. We have limousine service to take us home. Part of the service."

The door attendant has the taxi and complements them on their looks. "Ladies, how beautiful you are. I wish I were 55 years younger. I must pass it on to the younger generation. Good luck ladies, I know it will go your way."

They slide into the taxi carefully as miniskirts require. 35 minutes later, they are at the house, or estate may be a better word. They walk up the stairs to the entrance and Natasha signs in on the member book. Stella signs in on the guest form with Natasha signing in for the responsibility of the guest.

They enter the main lobby and look around. It is familiar to Natasha but overwhelming to Stella who pokes Natasha in the ribs with her elbow and whispers, "This is something. I've seen many of these people in the newspaper, television and movies. Ohh, there's a couple of athletes from the NHL. They are so immaculately dressed. This is a celebrity warehouse."

"It is. Wait till you go into the activity room. A large room with sofa, big chairs and a few beds and mattresses. Around the big room are private rooms for S & M, some bondage and whipping stations, straight sex rooms, gay and lesbian rooms and other desires."

"In time, I am going to try them all. I may not like it, but it must be tried to find out," an excited Stella responds with bubbling enthusiasm.

"Good girl. Let's go get'em."

They walk around the lobby meeting people. Stella is in awe. She gets to meet the hockey players where she babbles out, "I just love hockey, so fast, so smooth and yet almost violent. I love it. My husband introduced me to the game."

The athlete reaches into his pocket and pulls out two tickets with seats near the player's bench. "Take these and come to the game on the ticket's date. Best no husbands just you two and if you like, we can meet after the game." Natasha takes the ticket, Stella is spell bound and cannot move. If she is not careful, her eyes will pop out.

"Remember, Stella what happens here never leaves here. This rule is strictly enforced and it has never been broken, as we know so far. The risk is too great for anyone to blab."

They walk out of the main lobby and into the Naked Den, as it is often called to separate it from the lobby area.

Stella freezes, hand to mouth, eyes bulging. Men and women are moving around, chatting, caressing and patting each other while naked. Some are playfully chasing and giggling. Some are on the sofa in a tangle of arms, legs and bodies. Some are on the mattresses fucking like hell in pairs and groups. There is no inhibitions in the Naked Den. It is all free, consensual play.

Natasha leads Stella around to the private rooms to see the action. The first room has a woman with her ankles and feet tied to the bed. Four men and two women surround and molest her. She is in ecstasy, moaning, groaning and yelling for more.

The next room has one woman with three men filling all her orifices. She can only moan and groan, as her mouth is full. But, she is happy.

The next room has a man's hands tied to a hook hanging from the ceiling. He is stretched up with his feet one inch off the floor. A masked man, just like in the wrestling tag team matches is whipping him with a horse's crop and several other styles of whips.

The next room has women holding down a woman while another woman paddles her buttocks which are glowing red. Buttocks engorged with blood to stimulate the genital area for better orgasms.

The next room has a woman in chains submitting to the desires of several men.

"The next room is the role-playing room," Natasha informs Stella. "This room has a large closet with various clothes for different roles, like the playing of little school girl and big bad man, or the policeman with a prostitute. You think of your desire and this is the playing field to act it out."

"This room is for the gay men or the heterosexual men who want to give it a try."

"This room is for lesbian sex."

As they were almost at the end of the private room tour, the two hockey players approach Natasha and Stella.

Natasha talked with them for a few minutes and then excused herself. "I have some business to attend, can you guys look after Stella."

"We would be delighted."

She slowly walked away and then looked over her shoulder. Evidently, no time was wasted in taking care of her. Her clothes were being removed, her body was being massaged and kisses were reined all over her. She was now on her back with one hockey player in her vagina and one in her mouth.

"I guess she will be alright." Natasha said to herself.

At 7:30 am Natasha and Stella meet, or collided as both were weaving and wobbling trying to find their clothes. They looked at each other, smiled, giggled and together, "I'm done." They dressed and the limo drove them home.

THE CON MAN

9:30 am Brehtt wakes up, thinks about his readings on Titanic and says to himself:

> *"I can play right and left handed, and oddly enough, I am better at left handed then right handed. Time to play my idol."*

He dresses, munches on breakfast and drives to the Deep Hollow Country Club known for its money games. He parks, gets his clubs from the trunk and proceeds to the practice range, driving range or learning range. These names range among the golf courses in an attempt to sound more sophisticated but actually the people still call it a driving range.

Approaching the driving range mat area he looks around, not many people except his eye catches a beautiful swinger at the far end.

> *"This guy is good. He may just be one of the guys or knows of some of the guys who like to play for money, big money.*

He walks over and positions himself a few yards away to not distract the golfer. He hits a few shots with his seven iron to warm up and then goes with his driver. As planned, he hits a few beautiful slices or banana balls as they say. He grumbles, gives a few moans and then takes a break, sits down behind his station and watches his possible mark hit them long and straight. When the mark takes a short break Brehtt says, "You sure hit a nice ball. I've been trying, reading and studying and I still slice the damn ball."

The mark looks at him and says, "Yeah, you're just cutting across the ball to put a slice spin on the ball. Try holding you right shoulder back while the downswing begins. This helps to delay the shoulder action so the shoulders are square to the ball at impact. The right shoulder often spins around too fast for the hands to catch up and the lagging hands leaves the club face open and cuts across the ball, causing the slice."

Brehtt returns to hitting with a little better results, but not too much better. He is here to make money and not impress a stranger on the driving range.

"Thanks, I think you may be onto something. I've been watching you swing and I notice just what you said. The hands drop down before the right shoulder moves. I am going to practice this. By the way, my name is Brehtt Bennett, and yours is:"

"Sam Ryann, I am the pro here."

"Sam, I would like to get a game going, a money game. I am not that good yet, but I think I will be good shortly because it cannot be that hard a game. I would like to play for 20 dollars a hole. Since you know the members, maybe you can help me out."

"Well, most of the money players are out on the course already, but I'm free, and if we can make an amicable arrangement on the bets we can tee off in a few minutes."

"This is great, maybe I can learn a little. How 'bout you give me 3 stokes a hole for 20 dollars a hole."

"Oh no, I am thinking of one stroke a hole and on the par fives you get two strokes."

"Ok, good enough. Let's go. I am really anxious to get a game."

They tee off and the pro as usual was around par for each hole. Brehtt was just simply brilliant in looking like a beginner. His shots sliced, hooked, dibbled and at times, he even missed the ball. He kept a sense of humor when on the seventh tee box he missed the ball twice. He told Sam that he was not used to this course, as it was two inches lower than his home course. Sam just smiled wondering who is this idiot with the big ego.

After the 18th hole, Brehtt paid up and went to his car to put his clubs away. Slowly he returned to the dining area now filled with the early morning golfers. As he approached the entrance, he heard loud laughter and derogatory comments he did not understand until he saw Sam talking to the group. Sam was making fun of Brehtt and the easy money.

Oh boy, this is looking good. I have about 20 marks over there.

Over he walks to the group, who see him coming, and silence prevails. They are a little embarrassed but Brehtt puts them at ease with a little humor.

"I had a bad day, guys. My back was tight and sore like it usually is. My hands were swollen from ditch digging at home for two long days and those late night poker games didn't help. But I am better than this and if Sam would be willing we can do it again."

"I would like to, but I feel guilty about taking your money."

"Now you pissed me off. Forget the guilt. I will not feel guilty about taking your money. Why should you? Do you use guilt to hide your fear?"

Things are getting heated. This is what Brehtt wants. Peoples' thinking becomes clouded under anger.

"Ok, we play 1,000 dollars a hole. Put your 18,000 here with mine. This bet is between you and me. The winner of the most holes gets the 18,000. No strokes are given to either side. As for you guys, I will cover any bets you want to make. The rules are USGA rules. In fact, I will even play left handed to ease my back."

The guys are flabbergasted. Money this high is not unusual but it is unusual for a guy with Brehtt's caliber to bet even with the pro.

The money is flying. Brehtt is making notes as to who bets what. The total bets are at 100,350 dollars. The money is stored in the clubhouse safe and Brehtt has the club manager sign a contract that the money is in the safe for the winner. This is to prevent the club from confiscating the money.

The tee time is made for 10:35 the next day.

10:35 and Brehtt is sitting in a coffee shop, with breakfast about a mile from the golf course, thinking of his hero Titanic Thompson. He is doing the same thing Titanic does. He is going to be late. He is going to irritate the marks.

11:15 he arrives in the parking lot to the expected irritated fans and angry Sam Ryann, the pro. As expected, he gets the cackle of a chicken, "you scared," comments, "you asshole," "you hacker," etc.

"Boy, these guys are really riled. My type of marks."

There are no customary greetings or handshakes. They proceed to the first tee. Sam has the honors and goes first. He hits his drive, not a really a good one, but good enough considering his irritation. The ball is in the fairway. Brehtt hits and watches it sail over Sam's ball for another 75 yards. Sam is stunned as he mumbles under his breath, "Holy fuck, is this guy a hustler?"

Yes, Sam, he is. After 16 holes, Sam has finally given up although it showed after the first seven holes when he was down six strokes. Brehtt scooted along walking three inches off the ground. The other marks gradually migrated away from the match, knowing they were beaten. The only reward or satisfaction they may have had was calling Brehtt names, giving him the finger, etc. By the 18th hole, there were no fans or marks. They were defeated, beaten and mugged. They were finished.

Brehtt sunk his putt to end the match but Sam was not there when Brehtt turned to look for him to shake his hand. He stood alone and with great humble pride, walked into the clubhouse, got his money, $100,350 and drove off like the cowboys into the sunset.

CHAPTER 10

THE SPY LADY

Sunday they woke up in time for supper, but were too lazy to get up. No touching, no playing just talking. "Do you see your twin brother much?"

"Nahhh, like I said, he doesn't want to see me, so why would I."

"But he is your twin. There must be some connection between the two of you."

"When we were young we got along great but in the early teens we slowly drifted. I was having lots of sex and he had a girlfriend but no sex. Maybe he was jealous. I became a slut, whore, and trash in his eyes and so . . . let's forget it. Give me a nipple, baby."

Stella left for work on Monday morning, leaving Natasha in her usual late sleep-ins.

THE CON MAN

PYRAMIDS

Brehtt's cons are mostly bets or agreements. This way he feels that there is less chance of criminal intent. If a guy makes a bet and agrees to the bet then there is less chance of a lawsuit because it was an agreed arrangement.

This is why he stays away from Ponzi schemes, bogus stocks, bogus land sales, etc. because they are highly illegal and the scammers end up in jail very easily. Law enforcement agencies spare no time in hunting these frauds down.

Brehtt goes over these scams, enjoys them, but that is as far as it goes. He admires the scams, frauds and how they work. He admires the nerve, daring, impudence, audacity, and the balls these con people, men and women have, but he is not in love with their results of being jailed for their cons.

The simplest pyramid is the chain letter. Back in the middle 1900s, the chain letter was popular but has died a little recently.

> *"I got one a few years ago. Strangely, it was not for money it was for new golf balls. I was to follow the letter and receive many, many golf balls. Let's read a little more to see if it works."*

One receives a letter in the mail with instruction. There will be four spaces on the letter. Your name goes in space number one. And, the other names in the three other spaces. Number one goes to number two, number two goes to number three and number three goes to number four. Number four is out as he is already receiving his products.

Copies are made of this new letter, and you make many, usually 200 copies. The copies are now sent to various people. Many recommend purchasing a hot list of names that are reliable spenders. The hot list costs a few dollars but is recommended. The originators of the chain letter provide the hot list for more profit. You then mail the letter and the money or products roll in.

If you are lucky, you may make a couple of dollars or get a free product, but in most cases the cost of the copies, mailings, envelopes, etc. will not be covered. We can go into the mathematical formulas on the chain letter but it would be to no avail. No matter how hard you try and how many mailings you do, it does not work.

It does not work, so don't even try. Pyramid schemes are illegal. The Federal Post Office and many states forbid the practice of such schemes.

A poor man, Glenn W. Turner, was unsuccessful at many jobs until he pyramided a cosmetic company. On stage, he could whip up an audience. His pyramid sold shares in the company for 5,000 dollars. When a person bought into the company, he was then able to sell shares for 5,000 dollars and was able to keep a high percentage of the 5,000 before turning the rest over to Turner. Turner promoted the idea that one could easily earn 100,000 a year. Nobody did. One town of seven thousand people had one thousand distributers. Anyone can see it will not work.

In the early 1700s a Scotsman, John Law, a trained banker, fled England for France for killing a man in a duel over a woman. In France, he ends up as Controller-General of France's money. France was deep in debt from the wars and Louis XV's extravagance. John decided to float paper currency-government secured bank notes and create a national elastic monetary system. He restamped the coinage with half its weight in metal and yet kept its monetary value. He also invented the Mississippi Bubble, a phony stock company. Law had to escape the country when he was found out. His escape was so desperate that he had to leave great personal wealth behind to save his life.

This set the stage for the "copy cons" who also set up bogus stocks and bonds. A Robert Harley, the Lord High Treasurer of England, almost ruined England with his bogus sales. John Morris of America also went down with his corrupt Louisiana Lottery during the Civil War. Wilson and Addison were famous for their Florida land sale schemes.

William Franklin Miller, barely subsiding on low wages, made it known that he could provide investors with 10 percent interest on their money every week. This means 520 percent each year. Is this not "Too good to be true?" Everyone knows this rule, but greed, lust for money, easy money overtakes the brain and the investors walk, actually run to his door to invest.

The money was to be invested on Miller's decisions. He had free reign. In fact, his reign was so free he never invested any of it. He set up the Franklin Syndicate. Franklin was his middle name, and associated this name with the famous Ben Franklin. His goal was to make it the biggest syndicate on Wall Street to manipulate stocks. He thought big, and like all cons, he had one hell of an ego.

It was unbelievable how the money roared in from all over. He and his family lived in luxury, but they were careful not to disclose too much luxury to arouse suspicion. Suspicion was aroused. Miller fled to Montreal, Canada.

All these were forerunners to Charles Ponzi, of Boston, who like the others, manipulated investments with great promises. He took in a lot and paid out little in interest, but enough to keep the investor interested. His scam was almost identical to Miller's. Like Miller's scam, things became confusing. The investors are not making fantastic interest, so things broke down and suspicion is raised. Ponzi was arrested in Montreal, Canada after surviving for 15 years. He became so famous his name is synonymous with such schemes.

Although Miller led in the schemes, the Spanish Prisoner scam was operating back in the time of Sir Francis Drake. Like the Ponzi schemes, the chance for money, or greed would overtake the victims. The greed is often rationalized that things are legitimate, and the marks trust these people even though they are strangers.

The prisoner game starts with a wealthy person. Marks with money are better to work with. The letter to the mark is written by a person jailed unjustly. The jailed person has a vast wealth hidden in the USA and the jailers and prosecutors want the money. The mark on receiving the letter realizes that the jailed man is willing to share the money once it is recovered and if the mark is willing to look after the jailed man's attractive young daughter in the meantime.

> "The money looks good, but when you throw an attractive young woman into the pot, nothing could be better. Money and sex, even if the sex is imagined, is a deadly combination to bring any man to his knees," speculates Brehtt.

The name Spanish came from the scam of letters for money for ransom of the Spanish sailors imprisoned in English dungeons. These frauds progressed through the years to Mexico as the Mexican prisoner game. The incarcerated prisoner would use the letter to describe how he was able to sneak money, lots of it into the USA in false bottom trunks, secret compartments in suitcases, etc. Unfortunately, the trunks and suitcases were confiscated by the Mexican courts and were to be sold at public auction if a fine, usually 5,000 dollars or higher was not paid by a certain date, usually in two months.

To sweeten the pot, the jailed man offered his 18-year-old beautiful daughter, if the fine was paid. Usually a sexy picture of the daughter was enclosed. Here we go again – money and sex.

The letter also warned of secrecy for protection to him, the jailed man and the daughter. The mark was informed to go to Mexico and how he was to meet the contact man and a friend who was a guard at the prison and pick up the trunks and luggage to take back to the USA. The fortune would then be split.

As one analyzes this, it is difficult to imagine it working, but it did, and in unbelievable proportions. Wealthy people fell for it. Unfortunately, when they met the contact man things were so called dangerous as the mark was to be arrested as the government discovered the scam. However, the uniformed guard explained how he saved the trunks and the checks he was to receive, whisked him off across the border to go to the beautiful daughter's home to collect his part of the fortune. Of course, there was no daughter, no address, no cashing of bogus checks.

All these scams offer too good a deal. Too good to be true! After analyzing them, it is hard to believe they work and we wonder why. Remember, money and sex usually win out.

Brehtt laughs as he mulls over the Green Goods con. It started just after the Civil War in the USA when confusion prevailed from newly issued government treasury certificates and bank notes. The fraud was to actually sell counterfeit money at a cut-rate price, a price too good to be true. Letters, booklets and secret meetings were used to convince the marks. And, they were convinced. This was all a come-on to get the money and they did get the money and still sold no counterfeit bills. This con even resulted in confusion of the courts as counterfeit bills were not sold or manufactured. In many cases, the scammers got off lightly in that technically they did not break the law.

Along similar lines was the gold brick game born with the Gold Rush Fever. There were various formats to the con. The con artist posed as a miner, dressed and acted the part. With lead and gold paint, he made bricks to sell. He was in dire need of money for his debt in discovering his gold. Some even went so far as to set up a bogus assay office in which he took the mark to verify the authenticity of the brick. Naturally, the brick is valued at a high price like 10,000 dollars, but a quick sale is needed as the money is immediately needed, so it is sold at less than 10,000 dollars.

> "The old quick sale gimmick. Con artists do not want the marks to have too much time to think on the proposition because they may realize they are being conned. The old used car salesman saying that this car is being looked at by many so it won't last long. If you want it, you better move fast. Never buy anything under rush or pressure demands. This is why businesses have deadline for their sales, "Buy before . . ."

Repeatedly, we keep coming up with the simplicity of the frauds and yet how highly effective they are. Greed, voracity, lust, desire, hunger, etc. override the simplicity of the game. These emotions cloud reasoning.

"Ah, the psychology of it all. These con artists must understand human nature, and yet they have no degrees or certification in psychology, psychiatry or even sociology. Somehow, they know cognitive dissonance theory although they do not know it by name.

Cognitive dissonance is when the mind has two competing thoughts. Like people want a dish of ice cream but feel they should not have the ice cream. With conflicting thoughts, cognitive dissonance, the mind will often drift to the thought that will give pleasure. Even if you know the odds to the situation or if you know not to do this thought the tendency is to go with the one thought that will give you the most pleasure and satisfaction.

Cognitive dissonance is often the reason in betting. People will often bet against their judgment, the odds, and or simple facts, because they find greater pleasure and need if their bet against the odds does win. In casinos or in horse racing when things are down and the money low or gone, the bettor has conflicting thoughts in quitting or more bets. Usually they go with more bets.

CHAPTER 11

THE SPY LADY

Over the next two months, Stella tried all the private orgy rooms. She experienced just about all the sexual deviations other than the missionary position of which she was only familiar with. She was now as she claimed to Natasha, "I am now a wanton, perverted, whoring slut. I do not care what you call it. It is the new me, and I love it. Natasha, I love you so much for what you did for me."

"And now baby," thinks Natasha, "you are ready to supply CIA information without you realizing it."

"Stella, please tell me about your experience in one of the private rooms."

"Natasha, I thought I would try the bondage and S&M room. I went to the door, peaked in and a hand grabbed my arm. I was pulled in, stripped and tied up. My hands were over my head. I was raised up with just my toes touching the floor. Hands were all over me. Squeezing, rubbing, caressing, slapping and rubbing. They were gentle, but rough. It was scary, but exciting. I was fucked and sodomized at the same time. The penis in the ass hurt at first then eased off. In time, it felt good, probably because of the other penis in my cunt. At the same time, my nipples were pinched, pulled and sucked. Again, it felt good. I was then spanked, paddled and whipped. I had never felt this before. It was different somewhat exciting but questionable for the future. I really do not know if I can go with the pleasure and the pain together theory. Some people can. Some people seem to be most pleased when pain is part of the sex. I am not quite there yet, maybe, but not yet."

I like sex with you Natasha. It is all pleasure. The same pleasure with the two hockey players. This I like. I cannot say which is better, you or the hockey players. Both are excellent and different. So they cannot be compared. Four hands, two mouths, two cocks certainly doubles the pleasure. I also went to a private room to pull a chain of multiple men and women. Multiple partners, men and women, is great and I am glad I experienced it, but the one right person, like you Natasha, can still be considered the ultimate.

Natasha, I love and thank you so much. I am a slut, and a whore. I even talk like one now, using words like cunt, cock, tit, and asshole, instead of vagina, penis and breast and rectum."

"I am so happy for you," replies Natasha. "When your husband returns we will have to be a little more careful and we will not stop because you do not want to stop. When does he come back to the states?"

"This Thursday."

"How did things go over there?"

"Well, you know they were supposed to go to Syria according to the media and other sources but undercover they went to the Ukraine. This was a clandestine operation. They talked to the rebels and what their needs were. They coordinated plans with them. That is all I know. It is top secret and he may have told me more than he should've but I know it'll never go past you."

"Rollover, baby. I need more before Ralph gets home."

Later that day. "Brehtt! What are you doing here? Leave me alone. You don't like me and I don't like you. How did you find me?"

"I can always find you."

"I know, but I still worry about you. Your lifestyle is going to catch up with you. Sometimes sex can be dangerous and incurable. We don't get along but we still care for each other. If there is anything I can do just let me know. You know how to contact me. Take care. I believe in you."

He walks out the door. Natasha locks it. She is stunned by the sudden intrusion. He came out of nowhere. She becomes sullen, and despondent. She goes to bed. Cuddles up with herself in the fetal position and goes to sleep. This is her escape mechanism.

Natasha's cell phone rings to wake her up, "Natasha, I'm lonely. Can I come over? Ralph got an emergency call and he left, for Syria. Something happened in the Ukraine. The Russians somehow countered the U.S. plans in Ukraine. Somehow the Russians were aware."

"Yeah, glad to have your company. I feel lonely also. A little depressed. I talked with my brother. Nothing is any better."

THE CON MAN

Brehtt puts his history book of cons away and decides on what to do for the day. He cannot think of anything so he just locks up, gets in his car and drives off to a bar for a few beers and maybe some entertainment.

He walks into the Blue Eagle Bar, finds a stool and sits down at the bar. Orders a draft and looks around to see if anything is happening. Usual run of the mill. Talking, yelling, laughing, bragging, etc.

While looking at his beer, his neighbor leans over and says, "The pool table is open, if you play, care for a game?"

"Yeah."

They get up and go to the pool table where they play a friendly game. They play for an hour and finally the new friend asks if he would like to play for money since they seem to be of about equal ability."

> *"No way I am going to play this guy. I do not know him. He may be setting me up, this makes the betting uncertain. Remember, never bet unless you are certain of the outcome as my hero Titanic Thompson would say."*

"Nahh, I never play for money. I am not that good especially under pressure. Pool is just a time passer. But, if you like to bet I will put my martini glass on the edge of the pool table and place a coin in front of it and make the coin jump into the glass. I will not touch the coin with any part of my body. It's kind of an ESP thing."

"50 bucks if you do it and you give me $50 if you don't."

"For a guy who likes to play for money $50 is a little light."

"$200 same bet."

Brehtt takes the cue ball and lines up in a straight line to the coin. He strokes the ball, the ball hits the bumper in front of the coin, and the coin jumps up into the glass. Simple law of physics. The cue ball compresses the rubber pad upward at impact, forcing the coin into the air and into the glass.

As he collects the money he says, "Elementary, my dear Watson."

The mark is still astounded and replies, "You know it was worth the $200 because I learned something, and I will get that money back and much, much more doing it to others," and with a slight lowering of the voice and a soft smile, he says, "Just like you got me."

They shake hands and part.

Brehtt then looks around and a group of women are at a near table. They wave him over. The tall blonde-haired person says that they saw the action and thought it was neat.

"We heard you mention ESP. Are you really psychic?"

"Just in some things."

"We are skeptics. Can you show us something?"

"Let me sit down with you." They all squeeze over to give him room for close female companionship.

He thinks, or pretends to think and ponder, as he looks into each of their eyes. His thinking is not on ESP but on lust and desire as he looks into their eyes.

How about this? May I have the straw from your drink? Let's move the drinks out of the way for a little space. I will put the straw down here. Give me a minute to concentrate my powers and the straw will move across the table and I will not touch the straw.

With a minute of acting he takes his hand, points his finger and places the finger on the table about 4 inches behind the straw. He moves the finger away from the straw as if he is pulling the straw across the table. The ladies are amazed and delighted.

> "Again, the principal of simplicity," as Brehtt's mind evaluates. " It is not ESP. I blew the straw across the table by leaning in fairly close to the straw and lightly blowing at the straw. They see the straw move with the finger but cannot see the breath."

"What else can you do?"

"Ah, let's see. It is sometimes hard to come up with things. Ok, here is a mind thing that you ladies may already know but we will try it anyway."

A group of men are seated about 10 feet in front of 10 naked men and 10 naked women. Where do the men look first and why?"

"They look at the women first because they like tits and vagina, unless they are gay," was the first reply.

"They are not gay. They are heterosexual.

"They agree they look at the women first for the size of the breasts and hair on the vagina or lack of hair on the vagina."

"Sorry ladies, but the men look at the men first and look at their penises for a comparison with theirs."

"That's right," the quiet red head speaks up. "Men are always bragging about the size of their penis and are very proud of their penis and they are jealous of those with a bigger penis. They will not show their jealousy about the bigger penis guys so they will make fun of the bigger penis as a cover up to their jealousy and inadequacy. Ladies, get real. Don't men think they are great lovers and all that bullshit?"

Now the conversation gets interesting as sex and relationships are thrown out on the table.

"When it comes to sex, relationships and feelings, talk to women for better understanding. Women talk about feelings, emotions, desires, lust, love, etc. and all the ramifications of sexual emotions. These talks are fascinating. Men talk about how they performed, "I fucked the shit out of her. I did this, I did that." Men's talk is all about their performance. Men brag and assume the women were enthralled," as Brehtt's mind is thinking.

In time, the group dwindled with the blond and red head still at the table. The conversation is still on sex. Finally, the table goes into dead silence as the red head says, "With your ESP can you give me an orgasm. I've never had one."

Brehtt who was sipping his drink starts to choke. He coughs, wheezes and loses his breath but finally comes around. He looks at the red head and then the blonde who sputters out, "Me too."

Jesus Christ – did I hit the jackpot.

With no delay, "Yes, I think we can solve your problems. Your place or mine?

"Ours."

CHAPTER 12

THE SPY LADY

Stella arrives. They hug, kiss, sit down and talk. Natasha talks about Brehtt and how she wishes they had some kind of a relationship. Stella talks about Ralph who was very upset with the Russians countering their help to the Ukrainians. He is upset, but he knows such things do happen. Sometimes plans work, sometimes they don't. That's life.

Natasha is also relieved. She is confident that Stella knows nothing of her real job.

Stella spends the night with Natasha.

THE CON MAN

SEX THERAPY
They get to their apartment and Brehtt is shown around.

> *"Nice place, but only one bedroom. Are they lesbian or bi with some heterosexual thrown in? This is interesting. Oh well, let's see what happens."*

They all sit down on the couch where they continue with a few laughs, giggles and more drinks.

"Let's get busy on the reason we are here," interjects the red head. I am sure you noticed that we have only one bedroom. We both dated many men and had no success with them on the orgasm issue. We have nothing against men; it is just that they could not finish the job. We were always left hanging. A lot of it was enjoyable but we just wanted more."

"One day after work, we work for the same company," began the blonde, "we came here to make an elaborate dinner, just for the hell of it and to break the routine of ordinary meals. We had filet mignon, lobster, salad, cheesecake and wine, lots of wine, maybe too much wine. As we prepared the meal, we were prancing all over the kitchen, bumping and brushing each other as we made the preparation. As time went on, we were getting sloshed but having so much fun. One time we bumped into each other and we just stood there. No apologies or no excuses were made. We just stood there looking into each other's eyes. Why, I do not know why, I just said that felt good, it was enjoyable. She responded with I loved it too.

Then the world just stopped. We were magnets being pulled in closer and closer until our lips met, our eyes closed and the world just stopped. An atom bomb would not have changed anything. We hugged each other and shuffled into the bedroom where life changed forever. In time as we lay in each other's arms catching our breath, smoke was seeping into the bedroom. I screamed, she yelled, we jumped up in magnificent leaps, ran into the kitchen to see the filet mignon burning, the lobster burnt from the dry pot as the water was gone. The vegetables were also smoking, as the water was also gone. It was a fucking mess. Ironically, we just turned the stove off, left the kitchen, and went back to the bedroom to continue our romp.

We talked and it was the first time we experienced an orgasm. Soon my husband left me for another and took a job out of state. Her husband died from a drug overdose. It was only natural that we moved in together. The sex was good but we both felt that sex should be good even with men and orgasm should be possible even with men. Our past husbands were duds in bed, but not all men are duds. So far, we are unlucky with men and we are hoping the problem is not us."

"If you can help us even with your ESP we would like to experiment."

"The first thing you must realize is that sex is a brain thing and the brain must be receptive. People forget that the brain is the largest sex organ in the body. Getting the body ready means getting the brain ready first. Now, get out of your clothes. Getting the brain ready means really getting ready by strongly wanting. If you do not want sex then you will not respond as you should. Sometimes you may not be interested in sex but your mind can change with the proper seduction. Unfortunately, many men do not do the seduction slowly enough. The old slam, bang, thank you ma'am and that is it."

"The first move is often one of relaxation. Sometimes relaxation is helped with alcohol or drugs and sometimes they speed up the seduction. However, they are not needed. A complete relaxation can be achieved by some intimate kisses on the lips, neck, ears and on the cleavage area."

"I have to talk and do. As both are lying on their backs on the bed, I just keep on kissing them on the lips, neck, ears and cleavage. Just entice the breasts but do not move there yet as the momentum is

building. Some casual caresses of the breasts, ass cheeks, thighs help the process. The caressing of the skin is a big turn on in helping to build the anticipation of future delights. God, this is beautiful, so delightful. I have to stay in control."

"The next move is a big one, stretch her out and give her a full body massage, all the body, right from the feet to the scalp. The message is simple. Just stroke the skin towards the heart so the blood is speeded up in circulating the body."

"Nice smooth easy strokes. Light pressure strokes until later when heavier pressure is desired. My hands can usually tell by her response as to her desired pressure, if not, I ask. Vary the strokes from long languid strokes to circular strokes in some places. Use the heel of the palm and the fingers. Sometimes soft easy karate chops to the back and buttocks will turn them on. Some like slapping the ass to get the blood flowing in the area as a turn on."

Brehtt's mind is applying all the massage techniques. The women are becoming relaxed, completely relaxed, and very horny.

"Now is foreplay time. I run my palms up the legs to the vagina but do not touch the vagina. Massage all around it. The woman will respond to give you the message by moving her hips to your hands. Do not respond. Move to the other side of the vagina and as she moves to your hands switch sides again. Do not let her rush your response."

"Oh, fuck. This is so good. Finger fuck me. Do me. I need it. Quit your fucking playing and do me," the red head cries.

"In time my dear."

"Ahhh, she is getting ready. I am ready. My head drops to her vagina and the oral sex begins. She is squeezing my head, I can't

breathe, I am going to die in bliss. I can feel it coming and it does. I will keep using flat tongue strokes on her outer lips while pressing hard with my mouth. Then it's the tip of the tongue that goes into the vagina like a small penis. The tongue fucking then is replaced by licking the clitoris and with deep sucking and circular action. God, I wish my tongue was long enough to reach her G-spot. My finger moves into her vagina and strokes the G-spot located on the upper walls of the vagina, my finger is curled up towards the belly button. The rubbing and scratching is smooth and paced to her breathing. The breathing increases to a rapid fire pant. The tongue also speeds up its circular motion on her clitoris. The finger on the G-spot is still in action."

Her body arches up and then down, all over. Her legs are shaking and her feet are pounding the back of Brehtt. One good kick and he may have a spinal injury. His back is being scratched with those fucking long nails. Brehtt is taking a beating but it is so enjoyable that he feels like he is in bondage.

Soon she is dead. She is in her dream world.

Now is the denouement of lying back, staring at the ceiling and coming back to earth.

The roommate is now aghast in wonder. It is her turn. Brehtt takes a break. The two girls hug and kiss to stay in the mood. He kisses the blonde and goes through the previous routine. The massage is wonderful as there are now four hands working her body. Her anticipation is peaked as both the red head and Brehtt sense her readiness. She is ready so Brehtt goes down on the vagina; the red head is on the breasts. He tongues her the same as her roommate except he gives her the alphabet. This is when the tongue makes the letter A, then the Letter B, and continues through the alphabet. Since he made the letters as capital letters, he then repeats with the alphabet using small letters or lower case letters. He fingers her vagina and curls his index finger and middle finger up so as to reach the top of her vagina for the g-spot. He finds it and like a banshee, she is off shaking, groaning, and screaming.

Both women lay exhausted. Brehtt gets up to leave.

"Where are you going?"

"Home."

"You can't go now."

"Well, you wanted an orgasm. Nothing was said about fucking. You got your orgasm and I never even took off my clothes." Out the door he goes.

"Oh, fuck, that was good . . . for a man."

CHAPTER 13

THE SPY LADY

Natasha wakes up. Her head is pounding and slightly dizzy. This is not normal. She was good last night. Early to bed. Her mind is reeling with visions, mostly of her brother. She wishes she was closer to him. She loved him and the animosity is killing her. When they were young, they played together in childhood games and sports. As they grew older, the childhood games gave way to higher-level sports and adult pursuits. Brehtt taught Natasha magic, magic tricks, illusions and deception in the psychology of how to deceive people for control. It is kind of like controlling people by deceiving them with the magic of illusions and tricks. At fourteen years, Natasha discovered sex. Brehtt did not. With Natasha, the sex flourished. With Brehtt, sex stagnated. This was the beginning of their slow separation into a distant relationship.

Natasha now cried while in the fetal position on the bed. *"Why, why, I miss you so much. Please accept me the way I am. I accept your abstinent ways. Let's go back to our childhood." She continues to cry and sob quietly and drifts back into sleep, her reliable defense mechanism.*

THE CON MAN

TITANIC GETS CONNED
Brehtt spends the evening reading more on the con artists. Here are a stories he likes:

From Toledo, Ohio, Titanic decided to return to Hot Springs, Arkansas to spend some time with his wife. But, perhaps more importantly the word was out there was a big high roller game in Hot Springs. This he liked, so he got on a southbound train. As he settled in his seat, he heard his name being called. He turned around to see an old acquaintance coming down the aisle. It was Tony Rizzo, a former racketeer in New York. He sits down with Titanic and they talk. It seems the underworld people forced Rizzo out of business so he left New York for his and the family's safety. He was going to Hot Springs where he owned a restaurant.

Rizzo had a limited vocabulary as well as a limited intelligence outside of his racketeering business. As they talked, Titanic realized that Rizzo was absent a full deck, and so his mind moved fast in the possibility of using him for a con. After all, they were both going to be in Hot Springs. With a con formulating, Titanic says," Rizzo, does it bother you that you are so illiterate?"

"Jesus, Ti, it's not so bad, but what does illiterate mean?"

"It means you are not too smart in reading, writing and figuring things like numbers."

"How can you say that? I did all right in the past and still doing good in Hot Springs. I can't be that dumb."

"Ok, let's make a deal. I'll teach you a couple of ten letter words, and if you can still remember them when we get off the train I will give you money for the cost of your fare."

"Fair enough."

In a little time, Titanic developed the words 'rhinoceros' and 'anthropoid'.

> *"Those words are pretty good for a guy who had very little school learning."*

Throughout the trip, Rizzo was grilled on the words and their spelling. As they got off the train, Rizzo spelled to Titanic each letter of the words, "r-h-i-n-o-c-e-r-o-s . . . a-n-t-h-r-o-p-o-i-d.

"Brilliant and Titanic gave Risso the train fare money.

"Prior to their departures, Titanic told Rizzo, remember the spellings and when I see you again be ready to spell them for me."

"Come by the restaurant any time and try me."

"I will."

Titanic went into a downtown store looking around. He spies a sales clerk who looks like he may be just right. He buys a hat from him and asks him if he would be interested in playing a practical joke on some of his friends. For 50 dollars, the sales clerk agrees. Titanic tells him to memorize the five ten-letter words. Have dinner at the Rizzo restaurant, the new Italian restaurant about 8 o'clock. .

.

That evening many of the gamblers are there for the big crap game later that night. They are jovial and full of life. Seeing Rizzo at another table, Titanic says to the group, "You guys know that Rizzo is a cagey guy. He is not as dumb or stupid as he pretends to be. Actually, he is fairly smart and he acts dumb as a cover."

"Titanic, that's bullshit. The guy can't even write his own name. He is the dumbest man on the planet."

"No, you guys got him all wrong. I will bet he can spell any ten-letter words that you want."

They all laugh and joke.

"If you are serious, Ti, I will cover that bet with this 1,000 bill."

Titanic plays hesitant, "Well, maybe I . . .

"I want in," seems like a chorus as everyone in the group lays down 1000 dollars. 6,000 dollars is on the table and Titanic covers it.

Titanic knows that the gamblers are not too well versed on big words so he calls over his shill, the guy he bought the hat from, who was sitting nearby. The shill is dressed to perfection, ambles over to the table and shows a lot of class. Titanic says, "Young man, you appear to be a successful person and may be able to help us. May I ask your business?"

"I am a lawyer."

"Ah, very good. We have a debate here. Would you be able to write down five ten-letter words on this piece of paper?

The lawyer, actually the hat sales clerk, says no problem and writes down five ten-letter words that Titanic previously gave him. Naturally, he does a little humming and hawing so as not to make it look too easy.

"Thank you so much. Now let me take your meal check and I will pay for your dinner."

The shill feigns confusion and lack of understanding to throw any suspicion of association with Titanic. He goes back to his table but keeps looking over his shoulder to show confusion about the situation.

Titanic takes the list and they go over the words.

Restaurant
Cacciatore
Rhinoceros
Cannelloni
Anthropoid

Someone says scratch the first name as 'restaurant' is listed on the window.

Another one says no "dago or wop" dishes so 'cacciatore' and 'cannelloni' are out as Rizzo is Italian and just may know how to accidently spell those words.

"That leaves us with two words, Rhinoceros and Anthropoid. Now which word do you want to use?"

"One guy says, I never heard of the anthr . . ., the last word so let's use that one."

Titanic figures this is looking good. He gets the waiter to bring Rizzo over to the table. When Rizzo arrives, Titanic tells Rizzo that he was telling the boys how good you can spell and that you are intelligent.

"Rizzo, spell the word Anthropoid."

Rizzo beams. He is on stage, "R-h-i-n-o-c-e-r-o-u-s.

CHAPTER 14

THE SPY LADY

It was a tough night. Natasha cried herself to sleep. Woke up and cried herself back to sleep. The night was a repeat performance of crying and sleeping. She lazed around all day in kind of a daze. Finally, at 9:00 pm, worn out from feeling sorry for herself she dresses up spiffy. She is quickly out the door and out the main door exit. The doorman has hailed a taxi for her. She is on her way to an orgy, and hoping sex leaves the throbbing in her head and put her back to normality.

She quickly pays the taxi driver, gives him a big tip and hurries up the steps to the main entrance and into the main lobby. She looks around, says a few hellos gives a few waves and head straight to the bondage and S&M areas. *"I am going to get the shit beat out of me. . . I need to be punished. My behavior needs to be punished. Brehtt may be right. I should change my behavior but I can't. If Brehtt can accept my new behavior maybe I can change. Life was so much fun before we grew up."*

She barges through the S&M door. A woman on a mission. A woman trying to find a cure. "Okay ladies and gentlemen, do me good, fuck me, whip me, and punish me. Do not hold back. I am a bad girl. The group is familiar with these treatments. Within minutes, really seconds, she is stripped, tied up, gagged and blindfolded. She is hung from the ceiling, toes off the floor; she is paddled, whipped and scratched. Her nipples are brutally sucked, licked, pinched and sometimes softly licked. She moans, groans, whimpers, yells and screams.

"Why am I doing this? It hurts, the pain is unbearable, I don't like it but I need it. I am mixed up. No, I am fucked up. Maybe I should slit my wrists but if I do that, I will miss all the good sex of life. This bondage and S&M is the shits, I don't like it, but it may make me change my behavior for the better."

Natasha gets a sudden burst of energy and yells out, *"Harder you bastards, fuck me harder, whip me harder, and fill my holes harder. Punish me."*

Two hours later a beaten woman wobbles out of the room, with clothes in hand. Outside the private room she dresses. Her body is red, beaten with red and purple marks, scratch marks that have almost drawn blood. Methodically and slowly, she's out through the lobby, out the exit and down the stairs to the limousine to be driven home. On the way home, she is planning her defense mechanism. The old standby, curl up and go to sleep, curl up and go to sleep and all the pain will vanish.

THE CON MAN

SOMETIMES THE CON GETS CONNED
Brehtt wakes after a good night sleep.

> *"I think I will just go to the golf course for a round of golf, dinner and cards if available. This is my easy day. No work planned."*

Off he goes to the golf course, looks around for a game but a 14-year-old kid spots him. "Hey, Mr. Bennett, you got a game?"

"No."

"Can I play with you?"

"Sure, bring your golf car around and I will throw my clubs in."

He throws his clubs in and off they go.

"Mr. Bennett, my name is Will Stevens, but you can call me what the others call me – Scamy."

"Well, you call me Bennett or Ben."

At the first tee they do their meaningless usual get ready ritual. A few swings, a few stretches, etc. The kid drives first, a 'beaut', 240 yards and straight.

"How old are you."

"14."

"You're good kid, so far anyway."

Brehtt drives his usual 290, as there is no money on the line. He is just out for a little fun. The game goes along nicely. Both play well and Brehtt is amazed at the 14 year old who is just a little over 100 pounds and swings with good mechanics. At the 18th hole Scamy says, "Mr. Bennett, I have a swing technique where I can increase my drives immensely. I do not use it while I am playing because sometimes my control with it is bad. But, this is the last hole and I would like to bet you that with this new technique you cannot drive your ball past my ball in two strokes."

"Ok, how much, a dollar?"

"Mr. Bennett, a dollar is not a bet. A dollar cannot buy anything. How about 100 dollars."

"Do you have 100 dollars?"

"Yes, I have 100 dollars. In fact, I have 500 dollars in my pocket right now but I realize it may be a little steep for you?"

"*Who is this fucking kid? 500 dollars?*"

Brehtt should have realized something was up on the last hole when the kid starts to call him Mr. Bennett.

"*But, it's a fucking kid. What does he know about scams and cons?
I'll teach the little bastard.*"

"Ok, 500 dollars to you if I cannot hit my second shot past your first shot."

"*I will win this and give the money back to teach him a lesson.*"

Simon drives off number 18. The ball sails forever to 320 yards. He smiles a smug grin. "Show me what you got kid."

The kid tees his ball. He stands over it looking down the fairway, waggles, steps back and repeats his stance. Steps back but this time he stands to the opposite side of the ball to hit the ball backwards to another fairway. He hits it 250 yards. Brehtt's ball is now 570 yards away from Scamy's ball.

With open jaw, Brehtt is momentarily frozen, stunned, petrified and conned. He goes to the kid, gives him 500 dollars, and walks in to the parking lot with him. He is not mad at the kid; actually, he admires the kid. He underestimated the power of someone just because it was a kid. He learned a lesson. He was conned. He shakes hands with the kid with lots of praise for the kid. The kid took all his cash, so he goes home.

"Drop the 'y' and you got Scam. They call him Scamy."

The next day, Brehtt stays at home for a nice easy day of reading, eating, napping and doing nothing energetic or needed, like vacuuming the rug, house cleaning, etc. His reading is usually about sociology and psychology in regards to human behavior as it is how he earns a living. He interacts with people and the people give him money. He does not ask for the money. He just gives the person or people a choice – take the bet or leave it. There is no force, coercion, intimidation, or bullying. He knows how the person will react. It is human behavior.

As he relaxes, he contemplates:

> *"Well, I guess I am not in such bad company. Con games are all around us." Businesses, financial institutions, religions, the internet, are all utilizing scams, and they get away with. At least when I pull a scam, the target has a choice – take it or leave it.*
>
> *How 'bout Enron, and other banking and financial institutes. They manipulated money and mortgages to scam their investors and the government bails them out. Many times the CEO's just got retired with big bonus money. A similar operation on a small scale would*

send the people to jail. Maybe, just maybe, the bigger the scam the easier it is to get away with it. Is it fraud to say, "To big to fail," a common saying at the time, so they get a bail out?"

He now reads from his book:

With Christmas coming up the public is hit with a new toy, appliance, whatever. They make a need for this item. So with this great need the stores are undersupplied so they sell out early. Parents come in to buy the great toy only to find they are sold out. This means they have to buy other toys for Christmas. After Christmas, the public is hit again with new shipments of the toy. The kids demand the toy because it was promised for Christmas, and so the parents go and buy the new toy, which is abundant. The parents have to buy the toy to be consistent in their promises. The toy companies have conned the parents into more purchases by forcing them to buy replacement toys because they were 'sold out'. They were not sold out. They were just not 'putting out' the toy.

Businesses, manufacturers, and entrepreneurs do studies to devise ways to con you into feeling the need to purchase items, whether you need them or not. Their job is to make sales. We teach marketing in college as part of the business degree. We use psychology and sociology to find out if the ploy will work to increase sales. For example, Wal-Mart and other stores will have a "greeter" greet you as soon as you walk into the store and often will ask how you are feeling today. The store wants you to feel they are friendly with you and to make you feel good because their research claims people spend more money when they feel good.

After you pay the cashier for your purchase, the cashier will say, "Have a nice day." It is said often with no emotion of caring or sympathy, as the cashier is not even looking at you. It is an emotionless, "Have a nice day," said because the cashier was told she must say it.
Often, I've been paying a cashier and in conversation about the purchase she keeps interrupting me by yelling at customers entering the store, "Welcome to . . ." Like with no sincerity of the "nice day" comment. This is irritating but the research says it means more sales. It's driving me nuts.

Studies have been done where a solicitor would phone and ask if it would be ok to come by to sell some cookies for a charitable organization. The response was not very good. The experiment was repeated and the person was asked how they were feeling today. This simple question of one's feeling seems to show an interest in that person and this thoughtfulness doubled the response to buy the cookies.

Research has shown that people tend to spend more if they are happy, feel important, and welcomed to the store. Therefore, a greeter welcomes you at the entrance in the hope to make you feel good and spend more money. The USA is a spending nation, and even the government overspends. Maybe we need college courses to prevent people from falling into these spending traps. Advertising is just too good nowadays, and advertising is based on research on how to get more sales, how to con the people. Is credit card interest a scam?

Many companies use contests to promote commitments to their products. The contest entails in so many words or less finish the sentence, "I like this product because . . ." They give away good prizes and the expense of running the contest is high. The real purpose of the contest is to get commitment by the people. By entering and writing their endorsement, they become committed to the product. This commitment means more sales.

> "Well, I guess I am not in such bad company. Con games are all around us."

Salespeople use strategies to get commitments. Get the buyer to make a commitment. For example, let's look at the car salesperson.

"Do you like this car?"

If the mark answers yes, he has made a commitment. The salesperson then goes through many of the features the buyer may like, the interior, the color, the horsepower, on and on. Each feature brings a commitment.

"Would you buy this car if the price was good for you?"

Again, the yes is a commitment. Now the price comes up, and usually the car is bought.

> *"I'll be damned. That is so true. If I ask any person about the car they just bought they always say the price was too good to refuse or something to that effect. What they are saying is not that the price was right but that I made several commitments on liking this and that so the price went in line with what I liked or committed to. Actually, the price was irrelevant as the buyer talked himself into the purchase. The car salesperson just conned the buyer while the buyer drives away thinking he conned the salesperson. Is this what they mean with the silly "Win/win" situation?"*

Like many things, we start small and build up to the possible maximum. This principle works for the con man as many of the scams start small and escalate. Card games, three-card Monte, the shell games all start with small bets and increase as the game goes on. Winning a small bet brings in larger bets as the con man has helped the target gain confidence and a feeling of invincibility. Winning the small bets increases his commitment to play for larger bets. In poker, the ante is small but escalates with the expectations of the cardholders. There is a saying, "Be careful in agreeing or committing to small things as you many end up having committed yourself to larger things later."

Often, when a mark makes a commitment, they will stick to their commitment even when things go bad. They feel it is a matter of time for things to get better. Like a gambler's addiction, the next bet will be better and losses will be recovered. Quite often, the mark will not change his mind and get out before things keep getting worse. So many times the mark keeps being milked for more money, and the mark keeps playing because his mind says it will get better. He behaves consistently with his commitment. The con just loves these guys.

Sometimes these small commitments lead to a change in one's self-image, and the self-image leads the person into bigger commitments. A person watching three-card Monte enters the betting and wins his first bet. He bets again and wins. Now his self-image is that he is good and perceptive in his picking the right card. He is now hooked.

The stronger the effort the greater the commitment. People who go through a strong arduous initiation process make a stronger commitment to the group when it is over. Some say this is why Marines are so committed to the Corps even after they leave the Marines. In making an effort to be a Marine, they go through a rigorous boot camp and training. The Navy Seals, Green Berets, etc. go through a training program just short of human endurance that weeds out most of the soldiers. The ones that survive have a strong commitment to the group.

Mothers have a strong commitment to their children because of their great effort and pain in pregnancy and birth. Again, leading to strong commitment.

> Brehtt keeps reading on human behavior and recalling past experiences.

A woman in an abusive relationship will often not leave the abuser because of her feeling of commitment on religious vows, embarrassment or the fact that maybe it is her fault. Her reasons for maintaining her commitment are weak but she holds on to her belief.

Consistency is a desirable trait in people and people want to be consistent. Inconsistency in not a desirable trait as it shows a person of weak character, no direction, confused, two-faced, and even mentally ill. A mark in maintaining his consistency keeps trying to recover his losses, keeps betting with higher bets, to the delight of the con artist.

Being consistent in thought and action often means that issues do not have to be evaluated and analyzed. People do not want to analyze or think in some situations. The matter is quickly solved by relying on their commitment. These factors are beneficial to the con man. Once he gets the mark hooked, the mark will usually be consistent in his belief.

The con man knows this lack of wanting to think and analyze is what makes his scam work. The mark believes the smooth talk, because that is what the mark wants to believe. The con man's reasoning is so good, the mark just accepts it. Some thinkers and analyzers are exceptions to the "it's too good to be true" rule.

> *"What we are learning is that consistency is a double-edged sword, a pendulum that swings both ways, good and bad."*

CHAPTER 15

THE SPY LADY

The sleep defense mechanism worked. Natasha woke up, alert and with a smile on her face. She dressed in a T-shirt, shorts and sneakers. Like a bolt of lightning she was out the door, on the sidewalk and out for her run. A 7 mile run today, two more miles more than her usual, just because she feels good.

On her return to her apartment, she bends down while shutting the door to pick up a pale blue envelope. She sits down at the table, reads it, scans the pictures and gives it some serious thought. She is being put on double duty. Her relationship with Stella is to continue but her need with Stella is not as important as it once was but must continue for possible future information. What little information Stella did give, proved valuable to the Russian cause.

This new assignment would be dangerous. This assignment had a conflicting message. It is the assassination of a high-ranking politician. One of the few politicians she loved. She did love this one. He was a member of the orgy club. He was also one of the best partners she ever had sex with. In her business, you do not fall in love. Love makes assignments difficult. She knew this. She could just not help yourself. "Love fucks up so many things."

She has the assignment. She has to carry it out. This is her job. It creates more trauma. The trauma of her twin brother's love and her love for the politician she must kill. The trauma of the one man she ever physically loved and her emotional love for her twin brother. Her head starts pounding again. She goes to bed and relapses into her defense mechanisms.

THE CON MAN

CONNED AGAIN

The doorbell rings and Brehtt wakens from his interlude of visualizing his readings. He opens the door to see a beautiful young woman standing in a mini skirt and a halter-top covering her breasts only to leave the belly bare.

> *"Wow."*

"Hi, I'm doing a survey for my graduate work to help expenses. If you don't mind, can I ask you a few questions? It won't take long."

"Ahh, err, . . . okay. Do you want to come in?"

"That would be nice."

She takes a seat.

"Let's begin. About how many times a week do you eat out?"

"I'm not much for cooking, so I go out maybe five times a week for lunch and suppers. Breakfasts I eat at home."

"For suppers do you splurge with wine or other alcoholic beverages?"

"Most of the time, especially with dates."

"What about movies?"

I like movies but I rarely go alone to the cinema. It is much more enjoyable with a date. I do rent movies."

"Do you like concerts and do you go often?"

"Often with dates and we attend quite a few."

"I bet you like stage performances also?"

"Very much so."

"Sporting events. Do you attend some and do you participate in recreation events like golf, tennis, fishing, etc?"

"Yes, I play golf and tennis a lot."

"Now, Mr. Bennett if you will give me a few minutes I will give you your score."

There is a little scribbling with a few grunts of appreciation.

"Mr. Bennett it seems you are committed to many entertainment and dining experiences that you enjoy. From your answers, it appears you could save from 800 to 1,500 dollars a year by buying one of these coupon books that give you discounts to the many events. At 100 dollars for the coupon book, you will save over 700 dollars. Now is that not a good deal?"

"Ohh. . . I don't know. I really do not plan on buying a coupon book. I just . . ."

"But Mr. Bennett you just committed to me that you go to all those things frequently anyway so why not save over 700 dollars? It does not make sense?"

> *"God dam'it. She is right, but she is pushing me into buying the coupon book. I do not want to buy the book but it makes so much sense. This fucking broad has me by the balls."*

"Okay, I'll buy it."

ESP AGAIN

> *ESP worked last time, so let's give it a try again.*

Off he goes to a busy bar. He enters and as always, he looks around for the layout and how the traffic flows. By stationing within the traffic flow, it is easier to catch the interest of someone. After all, hiding in the corner will not bring the marks to you. Good cons have the mark come to them; rarely do they have to search. The con creates interest in various ways to attract the attention of people. Sometimes it will be playing at something that will catch the attention of someone. When someone shows interest, others see this and will often join in watching. Sometimes the person will just holler to his or her buddies to join them.

He sits at a table near the flow of traffic to the toilet. Pulls out a small note pad and does some figuring, nothing of value or importance, just something to look busy and create curiosity with passerby's going to the toilet.

A tall brunette goes by, stares at him, but keeps going, evidently to the washroom. Shortly she returns, looks again at the diligent work of Brehtt, stops and says, "Haven't you got that figured out yet?"

Brehtt gives a little chuckle and says, "I think I have. Just a quick check."

"What are you checking?"

I think I can give you the name of a person in the telephone book from the answer to a formula.

"How does that work?"

"All you have to do is pick three digits to start, rearrange them and I will pick a name in the phone book that applies to that number. It is not much of a problem if you have ESP skills."

"Hey guys, come here." A group of six women come over to Brehtt. The migration of the women brings the men into following to see what goes on. Over twenty patrons are crowded around. The trick is explained and as is usual in such circumstances a skeptic will say, "It can't be done."

Brehtt has them hooked. The more they believe it can't be done, the more certain Brehtt is that the money will come in. They are hooked.

Brehtt pulls out a 50-dollar bill and lays it on the table. Soon the money is piled on in a pile for 750 dollars.

"Okay," as he motions to the tall brunette, you started it all so you will do the math. Your name is Yvonne. "Here is my pencil and pad."

"Write down any three different digits. The same number cannot be used twice."

She writes 742.

"Now reverse the numbers."

She writes 2, 4, 7.

"Now subtract the smaller from the larger. If you are left with only two digits than add a zero in front of the two digits."

She writes 742 – 247 = 495.

"Now, take this new number after the subtraction, reverse it and add them."

She writes 495 + 594 = 1089.

"Now get the city phone book. The last half of your answer is 89 so go to page 89 of the city phone book. The phone book is brought over. Now the first half of your answer is 10 so count down ten names.

Here Brehtt goes into his act of intense concentration and a little hokey-pokey.

"The last name has to be . . . and the first name is . . .

"Little do they realize that the answer will always come out to 1089. All I do is look in the city phone book go to page 89, count ten names down, memorize the name, and the con is on."

Brehtt picks up the money and starts to walk out the door, away from the startled patrons.

"Hey guy," yells the tall brunette, "Wait for me."

RELIGION, SPIRITUALISM, OCCULT AND BELIEFS

Brehtt is watching TV, half-awake and half-asleep. The football game is over and a religious program is in full bloom. The program is enough to trigger his mind into experiences he is familiar with through his study of history. His mind goes back to the past as he nods and drops off to sleep and dreams as follows.

"With all our scientific resources, religion, spiritualism, the occult and other beliefs still prevail. Why do we fall for these beliefs when reason should not let us? What are we looking for? Is there something always better? Is it the belief that convinces the person or is it the person's unorganized or submissive mind with lack of reason that convinces the person?

Who knows the answer, even if there is an answer? Whatever, there are many answers. During the 70s Eastern religions came on strong and are still strong. Cults like the Moonies and Scientology came and slowly dissipated in many places although Scientology still has a few followers. In the eighties a wide variety of so-called Christian sects were founded with their believers moving into commune like quarters.

Slowly, superstitions and witchcraft became popular along with the planned and alien programs of UFO's and alien life, astrology, biorhythms, haunted houses, ghosts, etc. These programs and beliefs gave the people a chance to be part of a higher deity or power to control their lives. With their lives being controlled there is no need to think and look after themselves. It is all done for them. Astrology and biorhythms are good examples of giving them their plans.

This has laid the groundwork for the con artist. He can give something that person needs. Smooth talk and good analytic logic and such a person submits and is seduced. Not all are seduced but there are enough of them to keep the con man living in luxury."

He reflects on his readings."

Desperate people search and continually search for utopia. Is there a utopia or is utopia just an endless search? It really does not matter because the con is ready to end their search. The con has the answers. He can and often does give the belief he has direct communications with God or another God if necessary. No one knows who the real God is anyway so it works for the con. It worked for John Smith who led the people into Mormonism, as the followers did believe he was a messiah from God. He was not the only one.

How about the cults of Charles Manson and Jim Jones? These two were blessed with charisma and criminal intent. The charisma lures the victim and the criminal intent takes over. People fall for it and lose their money to these types of con artists. It is strange how people are lured to these sects and then give all their money and assets to the leader. They become penniless and now have to depend on the group for survival and by doing what the group leader says. They become trapped. Often these leaders are sexual perverts who prey on the group's children, women and some men.

Manson got his followers to murder people in the name of God. Jones got his followers to move out of the USA and drink to their death the Kool-Aid. It takes a strong belief to do these things.

The Christian church is not exempt from scams and frauds. After all, it is so easy for church people to defraud the congregation, as the followers believe the men and women of 'the cloth' would never do such a thing. They have confidence in their clergy. They are honest and good people, and yet, the confidence is what makes it so easy for the clergy to defraud. Remember the word 'confidence' is the full word for the 'con'. The scammer gains the mark's confidence for success.

When religion moves into financial business, religion often gets away from the real goal of spiritual guidance. Instead, this spiritual guidance is used to make more money. If they make more money, where does it go? A bigger church, more expensive paraphernalia like bigger and more expensive organs, expensive and elaborate pews and alters. Is this not getting away from the real goal? Expensive church items does not mean one is more religious or that God loves expensive items, but such logic does not prevail and the better items are still needed. Also, one has to notice how the religious TV leaders live in luxury. Is this not against religious doctrine.

Soon the expenses do not meet the budget. More money is needed. The church now goes into investments and other financial workings. Religion is now used to promote their religion or sect for financial gain and for the glory of God.

The Baptist Foundation of America swindled money for God's work. Their scheme was not honorable. It was a blatant scam. They issued 26 million in public notes to acquire subsidiaries. The notes were worthless but were accepted by leading lending institutions because it was the church. Bogus donations of assets, over appraised in value, were accepted. These assets were overvalued for tax benefits and deductions.

And yet, some members accepted this scam because it was for the good of the church and God's will.

How about the Denver pastor of a six-thousand-member Calvary Temple who built a financial empire that went bankrupt with 3,400 investors out 12 million dollars? He was convicted of securities fraud. Ah, in the name of God his membership never lessened. It was God's will and the preaching still went on. He did nothing wrong as he was working for the Church. His members still supported him. In fact, membership never lessened.

His reason for the scams was that God told him to expand his ministry. He was televising his sermons to many states and Europe to large audiences.

James Orsen "Jim" Baker the television 'televangelist', an Assemblies of God minister, a convicted felon, and a former host with his wife Tammy Faye Baker of The PTL Club, was a popular evangelical Christian television program. A sex scandal led to his resignation from the ministry. Subsequent revelations of accounting fraud brought about his imprisonment and divorce. He later remarried and returned to televangelism using his sins to claim spiritual rebirth. Christians seem to love a rebirth in someone. Ah, finally they see the light.

Another common scam, on record, was the church having their gambling nights with bingo, card games, roulette, and dice games, etc. Gambling was illegal but no action was taken against the churches because it was the church – home of God – gambling was ok within the confines of the church. These nights were highly profitable and the priest took his share, a good share, and a personal share for doing God's work.

What is interesting is that on regular church days, usually Sundays, the congregation was usually limited with few people but on gambling nights, the place would be jammed. Were they following their God, or following the bet for money? The church did not care. Money was to be made, and they did.

Fortunetellers have their own following. They are astrologers, palm readers, tarot readers, etc. They are the people associated to Gypsies. Gypsies are still part of the con schemes.

> "It seems to me that I read where Gypsy crime in the USA amounts to over 300 million in losses each year. In fact, the word 'gyp' means to 'cheat' and comes from the word 'gypsy'."

An interesting feature of a Gypsy scam is that the women are highly active, especially in the various forms of fortune telling. They are good at hooking the customer with small payments and then escalating payments as the hook sinks in and the line keeps going. The gypsies pass their skills down the hereditary line. Little girls are taught at a young age and they absorb so much in living amid the frauds as a way of life. It develops naturally. Like the con artist, they become excellent psychologists, especially in the skill of depicting when the mark is in trouble, unhappy or worried about something. Once they find the problem, they milk it good and for good money, even though they rarely solve the mark's problem.

Vulnerable marks are ones who have lost a loved one or spouse. In their bereavement, they will be taken through various steps that keep increasing with the demand for more money for contact with the deceased. Each time the victims increase their donation they believe it will work this time. It doesn't. The money increases as they keep getting closer to contact with the deceased. Various scams are used to create contact but they are just deceptions.

People actually believe that the gypsy or fortuneteller can make contact with a dead person. Does this belief stem from religious beliefs that one does not die but goes to heaven, or maybe hell, where they enjoy a better life? Since they are alive in heaven then contact may be possible. People fall for it.

Fortunetellers, seers, astrologers and mediums have admitted that they are amazed at the clients presenting so much information on themselves and their environment. A simple question will trigger more information than was needed to answer the question but is vital to the fortuneteller's analysis. It is like throwing fuel on the fire to put it out.

When troubled clients come to the fortuneteller, they reveal their problems. This is gold to the gypsy. They will discuss the problem, but it has no bearing on the solution. The gypsy now makes the discovery that the client is under an evil spell and there is no way this person can find relief. With all sincerity, the gypsy will say that for 500, 1,000, 1,500 dollars or whatever the need is, she is a problem solver and can lift the curse to free the victim.

Some future prognosticators would not give a rosy picture of the future. The rosy picture of the future is what the client wanted because things were presently not so good. Here the con looks good. A dreary, bad, and even a devastating future is predicted for the victim. The victim is now beside himself or herself and scared for the future. The hook is in and now comes the line of for 'X' number of dollars we can change your future. Come back tomorrow with the money and she will finish the job. It takes an overnight of work so she will start the process when you leave and tomorrow we can finish the job for a brilliant future. The 'X' number of dollars is determined by the psychic's ability to use the job, house, savings, car and anything that gives a picture of the wealth of the person. Higher the wealth, the more the fee. Some fees have been known to go into the six digits.

The séance is an old familiar con. Although not as common nowadays, it still has some supporters and believers. The séance can be performed singly or in a group. With a group, they all hold hands in the light of one candle.

The mystery of darkness or near darkness. One must not see too much.

Various mysteries occur, the hand of the fortune teller being guided by a mysterious force writing on paper, the unseen voices, strange tapping the medium interprets as messages are some of the experiences the victims encounter. It is interesting to note that all messages come from the spirit through the fortuneteller. There is no direct contact with the spirit by the client. This way the fortuneteller controls the messages and no surprises in the message can occur.

Often, the victims have said such experiences are very emotional, spooky, frightening, and scary. Some even felt it as a religious experience.

As for honor among thieves, the gypsies never steal among their own people but it is encouraged with others.

CHAPTER 16

THE LADY SPY

The sun set three hours ago. "I need therapy," moans Natasha. Shower, make-up and dress-up. Taxi to the orgy place. Strange, the orgy place has no name. It is just a building with no name. The members like it this way. The members just say, "I will meet you there. Or, be there at 9:30 pm. "There" is considered the name of the building. Non-members have no idea when they hear someone use the "THERE." The members like it this way as it gives a sense of secrecy, like being special.

Natasha is going "there". She needs therapy. She is a bundle of nerves as she quickly exits the taxi, tosses a 50-dollar bill to the driver, "Keep the change." Money means little. She needs therapy.

She enters the main lobby area and sits on the sofa. She looks around to see what action is available. She fails to notice a couple coming up behind her. The man leans over the back of the sofa, nuzzles her ear, gently spins her head around as he kisses her nape, lower chin and then full on the lips with a passion all too familiar to her. She moans and tries to repeat his name but her mouth is full of lips and tongue. The sofa now sags beside her. It is a new body. A hand slides into her cleavage and her breast is massaged. *My god, the therapy is working.*

She immediately knows her guests, Jim Sloan and Kelly Sloan. Jim releases her, moves to the front of the sofa, and faces Natasha but he is blocked by his wife who has taken control of Natasha with her hand still on the breast and her lips locked with Natasha's lips.

"I am so glad to see you guys. I need you both real bad."

"Oh, honey. We are here for you. Shall we get a private room?"
"Yes."

As they rise from the sofa, the two hockey players approach and give Natasha a hug and a short affectionate kiss. Natasha introduces them to the Sloan's. Jim had heard of them but never met them. Jim was excited at meeting the athletes as he was an old college hockey player at Harvard and still loves the game. Kelly was eager to meet them because they were athletes, in excellent physical shape for extended sex activities. Kelly, when also at Harvard, fucked almost every athlete in all the sports before her junior year, and then she was in a repeat performance. It was not love or anything but a project to see if she could do it. In the end she stuck with Jim, he was the best.

"Hey guys, you want to join us""

"Yeah, that'll be great. All five walk to the nearest private room. They have it all to themselves. They locked the door. Give each other a quick hug and a kiss, well actually a groping hug and a sloppy wet kiss. The mood has been set. Slowly, carefully, deliberately they take each other's clothes off and then all jump on the big double king-size bed and jump around like preteens. The two hockey players gang up on Kelly. This is not new to Kelly but it is still exciting and meaningful. She has an arm around the neck of each player and pulls them in tight, gives each of them a quick kiss and pushes one head to her breast and the other head to her vagina. Kelly is now into space. She is moaning, groaning and directing the heads of the two hockey players. "ahhhh, right there, keep going don't stop, faster, harder, ohhhh, my godddd, you guys are good. I want to see more of you guys, more often. I. . . ohhh is all she can say as she smashes the orgasm sound barrier. She now goes limp, but not for long.

While Kelly was coming back to normality, she was watching Natasha and Jim. Jim was lying on his back. Natasha was straddling him with her mouth on his penis driving him to paralysis. Kelly reached over, pulled her off Jim's penis, and gave her passionate kisses to her lips. Jim, not giving up, got on his knees, rolled between Natasha's legs and drove home. Kelly worked her lips down to Natasha's breasts to help Natasha reach her climax, which she did quickly. However, being physically fit she rolled over, took two quick breaths and attacked the hockey players with alternating blowjobs.

For the next three hours, it is hard to assume time spent when having so much fun. Around 5 am in the morning, worn out, they decided to go home.

When Natasha got home, she felt better, but she started to cry, I have to cry. She cannot kill Jim. It is just too emotional. She must find a way out. The Russian government does not accept failure. The covers are pulled up over her head in a weak attempt to hide from the world and her assignment. Despite the trauma, she falls asleep, in her defense mechanism pose.

THE CON MAN

After his round of golf, he collects $655 in bets. Brehtt agrees to buy the drinks and hamburgers for the three in the game. They all sit down, order and continue the trash talk with bravado comments of what could have happened and what did happen. If these guys could live up to their expectations they would be on the PGA tour. The PGA tour is on the Golf Channel and so they watch a little and talk a little. The drinks come so they now add a little drinking to the talk. A golfer is in the lead by one stroke, hooks his drive into the water for stroke and distance penalty. The golfers watch and comment, "You choker." "A wide fairway to the right and you hook to the left." "You brainless motherfucker." These guys are in high-speed trash talk.

> *"What's with these guys? They have trouble breaking 90 and they criticize the pros. Each one of these guys had one or two penalties with out of bounds and lost balls. One guy had six penalty strokes for his round and he seems to be the most vocal in trash talking the pros."*

Brehtt gets up and without being seen he gets the waiter and tells him to delay bringing out the food until he gets the signal from him. If the cook has not started the order, have him delay it also.

Brehtt returns to his seat and orders more drinks for the group.

> *"The boys are really worked up by now. More drinks will set them up as they are hungry after their round. The alcohol is working on their empty stomachs and they are getting sloshed quickly. It's time now."*

Brehtt goes to the bar and gets a bottle cap from a beer bottle. He puts it in his pocket and returns to his seat. One of the players has finished his brandy so Brehtt reaches over and takes the empty brandy snifter.

"The brandy snifter is ideal," thinks Brehtt. The mouth of the glass is smaller than the body of the glass so that the center of the glass has a larger circumference than the mouth of the glass."

"Brehtt takes the bottle cap out of his pocket and while the guys are watching TV, trash talking and bragging, he places the bottle cap on the table, and moves the ash tray to within on foot of the bottle cap. He sits the brandy snifter between the two objects and stares at the set-up. He says nothing, but soon...

"What the hell you staring at?"

Brehtt hesitates with a little grunt, "Is it possible to pick up the bottle cap and deposit it in the ash tray by only using the brandy snifter, no hands or anything else?"

"Shit, yeah." Says one guy who is followed by similar comments from the others.

"I got 50 that says you cannot do it."

"I'll put 100 down if you got the guts to cover it."

"If you are so sure, I will go 200."

"Fine, here's my 200. Cover me."

Brehtt covers his 200 and says, "Anybody else want in?"

The money flows onto the table. Some bet 100 some 50. Brehtt covers it all. Nine people bet 200 and three bet 50 for a total of 3,950 dollars on the table.

"God, I love these country club members with money and egos to match. This is going to be a big day."

They all try. They try to slip the glass under the cap with a strong force to slide under the cap and into the bottle. They try flipping the cap up with the mouth of the snifter. Nothing works. After they have given up, they look at Brehtt.

Brehtt takes the snifter, places it upside down over the cap with the mouth enclosing the cap. He then swirls the snifter fast around the cap so that the cap spins around the mouth of the glass. Soon the cap rises inside the glass and spins around. He keeps spinning the glass and slowly raises it. The cap continues to spin inside the glass as he moves the glass over the ashtray, stops spinning the glass and the cap falls into the ashtray.

Brehtt picks up the money and as he is leaving:

"Thank you for the game and your meal is already paid for so enjoy the rest of the day."

THE MARK
The mark is the person targeted by the con artist.

> "How does a person or group of people become a mark? I just conned a group of golfers on the golf course and dining room. Why and how are they lulled into the con? Looking back at my marks, I study them to better understand why I was successful."

The con artist can be thought of as similar to the mark. It sounds crazy but it is true. The con's desire is to make money, easy money and lots of it. The mark seeing the situation is seeing the same thing. He also wants to make money, easy money and lots of it. The con knows his scam may be illegal or close to it. The mark sees it as possibly illegal but he still wants in. In fact, in many of the investment scams, the con artist will even tell the mark to keep this quiet, do not tell anyone, especially the police. The mark naturally will not tell anyone because he does not care if someone else is stung or if the money is illegal. The mark just wants the money.

The con artist and the mark both have a high degree of their own intelligence. Both have a greed complex. Money, more money or something of value, but the con may have a better psychological training and experience.

A scam is never realized until it is too late. Ponzi schemes and other investment schemes have run for years. When the fraud is revealed people cannot believe that such people fell for the scam. They claim it is so obvious, but it is easy to make this assumption after the fact.

People who are scammed are not stupid, ignorant, or just plain dumb. Actually, many marks are educated, and even highly educated. Con guys like marks with some intelligence because they can easily see the working of the scams and it looks good to their analysis. Some cons claim that it is integrity a little more than intelligence.

A mark, lacking in intelligence, often has difficulty in understanding the procedure, and may just mess up the whole set-up at a critical time. Also, such a mark may also forget some procedure and reveal the fraud. In scams, timing in various procedures can be critical and a bungling idiot can mess up the whole affair. When cons suspect this, even if the suspicion is low, they will walk away. It is not worth the risk.

Outside of bar bets and small cons the desirable mark is usually wealthy to a certain extent. Why not con the rich and make more money? People with money often have a sense that they are experts in finances. It they have a few stocks that are doing well their confidence goes up in thinking they are money wizards. They know how to spot a good investment and small bar bets are considered investments also.

Businessmen are ideal marks for such reasoning. They run a business so they think they know finances and economics. The majority of marks who are taken by big time con men are businessmen. These marks have the money for major investments, and if they do not have the money readily, they can raise the money with their contacts. They will raise the money because the deal is just too good to pass on.

Doctors, lawyers, dentists, university professors and other professional people are also high on the scale as marks because they have the money and think because they have a higher degree in their area of study it makes them intelligent and smart in everything.

> *"I remember one dentist in New York who was taken many times by con men and yet kept coming back for more. He became a steady mark for many con men who would recommend this mark to other cons. This is strange."*

Strange as it may seem, bankers are ideal marks, probably because they think they are knowledgeable in finances. Along with their knowledge of finances, they are also ideal marks because of their ready funds at the bank. Again, we have people who take out the money from the bank with the understanding that it goes back after the score. Sometimes, if a mark expresses an interest, the con will encourage him to talk with his banker. Sometimes the mark may even bring the banker along and now the con has two marks.

Even though farmers, ranchers and fruit growers seem to be away from the heavy people traffic they are good marks. Ropers go out of the cities to look for marks and "rope" or bring them back to the can man.

> *"I can remember on Saturday nights in North Dakota the wheat farmers would have their poker games. The pots often exceeded many thousands of dollars so the money is there. A spawning ground for the con artists."*

Police officers have also been victims of cons. One thinks that the police would be wise to the con but they are like the rest of the people, they want easy money.

A mark with access to funds is a prime source to the con. These people are in charge of estates, trustees, guardians of trust funds. Let's not forget the churches. They have the funds, and many church people have taken from the church as we have shown earlier. Often they borrow from these funds planning to pay them back when the big score comes along, or is supposed to come along, but the big score never comes.

Women are good marks, especially middle-aged women looking for more excitement in life with more money to help. Widows become very susceptible as they are lonely, and the con gives them companionship, love and sex. For this, the widow pays for the courtship and in the end when she is hit with the big sting of giving the con a loan, or giving him expensive gifts. She is in love and vulnerable. Before she knows it, she never sees the guy again. It is sad.

THE ROPER

This person goes out to 'rope' or 'lasso' a mark for the con man. Ropers work where money is plentiful. These big cons have other workers called the 'insiders' and 'outsiders'. These cons are quite extensive. The insider is also called the insideman who takes the mark from the roper and works with the mark further with more elaborate information. The outsider or outsideman is the guy who brings the mark to the con artist for further information.

'Ropers' are the guys that go out and look for these money marks. They are good at it. They find the marks in bars, stores, any area where people congregate. They talk to anyone, and everyone, looking for leads and they get them. Their charming ways bring the mark into the fold.

Ropers are good at getting information. They are glib and smooth. They know how to ask questions without giving the feeling of being too personal with a stranger. He also knows how to listen to the potential mark and analyze the things left unsaid. By listening, the roper gets all the information he needs as potential marks love to talk about themselves. It is a fact that people will talk more about themselves to strangers than close friends. This information often reveals future marks. A roper is one hell of a psychologist.

Resorts, cruises, vacations areas, expensive hotels, and spas are good hunting grounds for the roper. These people have money, and people on vacations often feel freer in spending money. Golf courses and country clubs are also extra good for cons. Some games are for very high stakes, and after the golf games there are the high stakes card games, craps and other money games. Titanic Thompson, perhaps the greatest of con men, spent most of his time in these places because the money was there. Ropers, insidemen, outsidemen, and the con artists follow the money.

Ropers have contacts all over the country who pass on information on possible marks. For this service, the contact receives a commission or straight fee depending on the mode of operation. Sometimes these contacts will learn the full operation and start out on their own.

Here is an interesting experience. Some people recommend a mark to the roper. Often this is a revenge against the potential mark. He may not like the guy for almost any reason, so he wants the possible mark scammed. It works better than killing the guy or physically injuring him.. The guy may not be injured physically, but he can be injured mentally as his life may well be ruined as all his money is gone, his family is gone and his job may be gone, especially if he was embezzling for money to pay the con. Sometimes a mark, who was taken for a considerable sum of money, will recommend a potential mark to a con artist for revenge of someone he does not like. 'If I was taken, I will see that he is taken also.' The revenge attitude is so strong that the guy doing the recommendation will ask for no commission.

One person in the safe manufacturing business was able to find wealthy marks because people who need safes are wealthy. These wealthy people were excellent marks, and so he received a high commission of 30 percent when the usual commission was 10 percent.

Some ropers use the newspapers to place an ad for business. The ad will read something to the effect that a business is looking for honest, reliable, and possibly experienced businessmen with 20,000 to invest for a large return.

"Ah, yes. The word honest is a come-on into the ad. This word is used verbally and now in text form. The use of the word honesty conveys the message that this is an honest business deal. They are

looking for an honest person because the business is honest. Reliable and experienced are also come-on words as the reader of the ad sees himself as honest, reliable and experienced. Many readers are not experienced but they think they are, so the ad works. The power of words."

Con men feel that their marks have a bit of larceny in them. Again, we are back to the similarity of the mark and the con man. Both are looking for easy money. The con man has no emotional ties with his mark, and the mark has no emotional ties for anyone who is going to get stung by the scam. Easy money controls one's emotions, and the con man is the expert in using this larceny, even just a little bit of it, to his advantage.

Interviews to people who answered the ad will stress the honesty factor of the interviewer and the proposed business deal. This is the big hook – everything is upright and honest and if this is believed then the fraud is on its way to success.

Ropers love it when the potential mark talks and verifies his honesty. Many times, such procedure by the mark is to convince himself that he is honest. In fact, a mark's honesty is a standing joke amongst the grafters and con men. The mark's unshakable attitude in his honesty, and integrity, leads the con in defrauding the mark.

"So true, so true. Marks are the biggest liars. They all lie. This makes it so easy for me. As a con man, I am well versed in lying and so I can spot the liars easily. Again, lying is part of the con. The similarity with the con artist and the mark comes out in the biggest con in the world – the art of seduction, the dating game, and relationships. Here we have two people, together on a date. Each is on their best or model of behavior. Each is trying to please the other, usually for ulterior motives. One is being nice for the chance of sex and the other being nice for another date. Ironically, they also may be out for the same thing: sex. The man wants the sex and sweet talks, moves slowly, uses flattery, etc. The woman may also want the sex but must act with reserve, no rush, I will let him think

he talked and persuaded me into it. If I give in too easily he may think I am a slut or a whore. I may be a slut but I must not let him think that I am. I can con him as he is trying to con me."

The seduction plays out – some wins, some losses in this face-to-face relationship. How about internet dating? This is the big con. No one knows what's on the other end of the email message. It could be a man or woman, a pedophile, pervert, killer, etc. – you name it. The text message can be an elaborate con of words, good words, choice words and convincing words. Words designed to create a desired image that will seduce the receiver. The message may be a fantasy one has of himself or herself. A fantasy at a higher level than their real self. The message and the reply message is often a skill in self-promotion.

Sometimes, perhaps many times, the message leads to disappointment when the real self is shown in person or revealed through a message mistake. When the message leads to a meeting the term blind date may become real as one finds the real person and the message are not the same. The con has worked until they meet.

Seduction, dating and relationship cons make it difficult to see the real person. Such things, like good behavior, being nice, considerate, etc. can lead to marriage where one finds that after marriage the person may not be the same person as prior to marriage. For example, the quiet woman becomes a loud nagger. The dashing man becomes a lazy, unshaven bum once married. Why not, the game is over, I can become myself. No longer do I have to act the nice person. No longer do I have to impress the spouse.

The ideal spouse before marriage is often not the ideal spouse after marriage because marriage means the con game is over. I do not have to be as nice and accommodating as before marriage. The dating con has led to a happy marriage, then an unhappy marriage, and on to often divorce.

Divorce rates are high, anywhere between 60 and 70 percent and, of these percentages, the happy marriage is in the low percentages. Statistics verify that marriage is not a successful venture. It is not even a 50-50 event. In a Seinfeld TV episode, Seinfeld said that he did not like going to weddings, as the odds of the marriage lasting are not good. At least if I go to the divorce proceedings I know it is final.

The chances of a happy marriage are not great. Why? When a con scams a mark, the mark is not happy. The mark is unhappy because he did not get what he or she wanted. Loss of money and time leaves the mark frustrated and embarrassed. It is the same when the marriage is taken under false pretenses as each played the con game of acting with a different persona instead of being themselves. Seduction, dating and relationships would play out so much better if the person would act and behave with their real personality. Oh well, that's the way I see it.

Marks often do not really know or understand how they were stung. If they go to the police, their story is not too well conveyed. This lack of accuracy in their story makes it difficult for the police to give good help. In many cases, the mark will not go to the police, as he is too embarrassed.

Not everything goes easy. Con artists must be prepared for the mark that loses his cool when he realizes that he has been scammed. This realization is not always at the end of the scam. It can happen anytime during the scam. Some go violent. Some breakdown crying and sobbing. Some just go comatose or brain dead. However, the ones that are dangerous are the ones that laugh it off. The laugh is a cover up to later violence. This is why con artists do not stick around after the scam. They get out of town, out of state, and even out of country. Some marks, the laughing marks, have been known to track the con down, kill them, attempt to kill them, beat them to an inch of their life or worst of all commit violence to the con's family. When people lose their money they can become mean and dangerous and plot revenge with great detail, much like the preparation of the scam.

It is amazing how some marks are conned repeatedly. Why, is the big question? Is it the personality of the person who feels that it cannot happen again? Yet it does.

"This is so true. I have conned the same people many times and yet one would think they would stay away from me. No, they come back and try to outwit me."

For example, the Big Alabama Kid tells of a mark he took for 50,000 dollars in Miami. The mark looked good for another play so they sent him to Vancouver, B.C. in Canada to get some more money. His banker tells him it is a swindle and will not give him the money. He waits in Vancouver for three months for the banker to forget the money. After three months, the mark withdrew the money and returned to Miami to correct the mistake that must have occurred on his previous investment. This returning to the con artist to try again is common and so the con artist will always give the con or a different con again to the same guy. The con artists actually believe that once they get a mark they have him for future cons.

Sometimes marks have been told by the con people that he was taken. For some reason, they get more money for a retry as it will still work and I want more money. Hard to believe but true. Some marks believe the game is on the level and see the opening they need to win it, but they never do. Reasoning and logic are not used.

DO NOT TRUST THE BET
An old guy is sitting at the end of the bar. The place is not crowed so Brehtt walks in and takes a stool not too far from the old guy. Nothing unusual as old guys are often sitting at ends of the bar. In time, with no conversation going, all sitting, and staring ahead like in all quiet bars, the old guy leans towards Brehtt and says, "I bet you 20 dollars that I can bite my eye."

Brehtt knows something is up, but for 20 bucks, he wants to see this as a learning experience. The bet is made.

The old guy removes his glass eye and bites it and then replaces it. Brehtt sees the con, enjoyed it and yielded his money.

With more silence and starring ahead, the old guy leans forward and says, "For twenty bucks I bet you I can bite my other eye."

Brehtt now realizes that the man cannot be blind because of his movements and previous walking to the toilet. If this is another learning experience, it is going to be a revelation, a dandy. The bets are made. The old guy opens his mouth and takes out his false teeth, hold it up to his other eye and bites it.

Again, Brehtt yields his money, looks at the old guy, gives a little giggle and knows he was taken but only for 40 dollars.

> "If this guy knew how to work a scam he should be better than 40 dollars. He has the basic equipment. His presentation needs work."

Brehtt then takes him into a corner of the bar and tells him how to delay the presentation to increase interest and anticipation of the mark. By not rushing, other people will notice the action and will want to get in on the action. This way he gets more bets and more money. The old guy listens and ponders.

"Okay, old guy, watch this."

They return to the bar, which is filling up fast, but they get two stools together. They order drinks and enjoy themselves talking and laughing. Brehtt asks the bartender for a glass of water with ice in it. The water is placed in front of Brehtt who looks at it and asks the old guy if he can lasso an ice cube with this piece of string.

> "Con men are always prepared. He has the string in his pocket for such emergencies. The string is of cotton, which is fibrous so that it will absorb the water. Synthetic string or thread will not work."

Brehtt makes a one or two-inch loop at the end of the string. The ice has to be in cubes and it is in bars. He then gives the string to the old guy and he tries to lasso the ice cube to pull it out. He is not successful. He keeps trying and draws attention to his attempts.

"Hey, old guy, what you trying to do?" a stranger asks.

"I'm trying to lasso an ice cube and lift it out."

"Jesus, old guy. Are you the stupidest guy in the world?"

This loud mouth is just doing what Brehtt and the old guy want. A crowd gathers.

"Okay, loud mouth can you do it?"

"It can't be done."

"Well, for a guy with so much mouth and certainty I think it can be done. Here's 100 dollars on the table, can you match it?"

"You damn right sucker. Anybody else want in this money maker""

The money piles up. 15 bets ranging from 20 to 100 dollars are on the bar counter.

The old guy gives the string to the loud mouth. He tries but is unsuccessful. Several others try with the same result. The loud mouth reaches for the money but the old guy grabs his arm.

"Hold on, it's my turn"

The old guy takes the piece of string and lays it flat on the ice cube floating on top of the water. Since food is served at the bar he takes the salt shaker and pinches a little salt on the string lying flat on the ice cube, and waits a few minutes

"You waiting for divine intervention?" laughs the loud mouth.

"No, I am waiting for the laws of physics to take effect, and if you kept that big mouth of yours shut during science class you never would have made the bet."

The old guy now pulls the ice cube out of the water. Picks up the money and with Brehtt walks out to a stunned crowd.

"The salt helps to freeze the string to the ice cube by letting the salt melt some of the ice and then refreezing around the string."

Outside the old guy thanks Brehtt for the lesson. They walk across the street to another bar. They get to the door and Brehtt says go get'em. The old guy walks in but Brehtt stays outside so they are not seen together.

After thirty minutes, Brehtt goes in and sees a big crowd around a table. He goes over. The old guy has learned how to draw a crowd. There is a pile of money on the table. The old guy looks up and catches the eye of Brehtt. Nothing said. Nothing has to be said. The look on the old man's face says it all. Brehtt smiles knowing the old guy is happy as hell. He walks out. He did not make any money today but he did help someone.

"Is this community service????"

CHAPTER 17

THE CON LADY

Natasha is depressed. Clinically depressed, no. Emotionally depressed, yes. She puttered around all morning, dressing slowly, no make-up, and just a quick brush of the hair. She leaves the apartment. Down the hall stairs, and outdoors. The doorman has a taxi for her. Her trip is to the Senate building. Where she walks around studying the environment. She is trying to get a feel for the area where Jim Sloan works. She is oblivious to all the hustle and bustle going on around her. Her mind is on Jim and Kelly. Why, why does she have to kill him? No reason is given. Why is he a threat to the Russians? Wearily, she proceeds scanning the buildings, the lobbies, the sidewalks, the office buildings, and mostly of all the scanning entails security. Where are the police? Are their cars prevalent and near at hand? Where are most of the people congregating? Are they moving alone or in groups? Are they being led into and around the senator's offices? She even looks overhead for any helicopters. These procedures are not new to her she was well trained in them. Little things like even where the dumpsters are located, are there any food carts around and if so where are they located? The mind must see everything and the brain must register everything. Details, and then detailing the details for any specific observation that might go unnoticed. Small details and things that were unnoticed can trigger disaster. Nothing is taken as unimportant. Everything is important. Mix-ups, foul-ups, mistakes and errors often occur and have proven deadly.

A highly trained mind is making an assessment that tells her this may not be a good area for killing. This assumption may change in time. The one advantage of using this area for killing is the crowding of people would be taken by surprise and would panic creating chaos and havoc. Mobs of people in panic could be an advantage for an assassination. As soon as the people hear a gun shot, its loud noise being familiar to most people, would immediately set off the panic. Now, with a little further thought, do not use a gun. The sound of the gun immediately triggers the area in the direction of the shot. Police and security would immediately move to the area of the sound. This may well hamper the escape.

Ahhh, why use a gun? A poison dart from a blowgun would not reveal direction of the attack. The dart would lodge in the neck; the target would reach back simply to scratch the neck thinking it was a flying insect or something immaterial and proceed with a few more steps. Then the target would crumble to the ground - dead. When the dart hits the neck and the target collapses to the ground, the assassin is on her way escaping. The assassin walks away free and easy. Some may stick around just to see what happens. This can be risky as police often scout a crowd after such actions because many assassins often want to see what happens and what develops. Curiosity can kill the cat. If the assassin had used a gun and police moved to the area of the gun sound, the assassin would have to move extremely fast to get out of the area. Anyone moving extremely fast in such a situation may be readily noticed. The blowgun can be used at a distance, which could be an advantage but people could also see it.

Perhaps, an old Russian trick of using a walking cane with a poison tip is most effective and unnoticeable. The assassin simply stabs the person in the leg as they are walking. The assassin simply closes in on the target and the walking cane simply touches the target's leg. On contact the poison is released from of the end of the cane. The release is by the trigger in the handle of the cane. After the release of the poison, the assassin simply moves on out of the way and the target after about 10 to 15 seconds falls over dead. The assassin is long gone and is unnoticed.

It is getting late and the sun has set several hours ago. Natasha is tired. Hails a taxi and goes home. However, her mind is still confused and even terrorized at the thought of having to kill someone she does not want to kill. "How can I get out of this? How can I get out of this?"

THE CON MAN

TITANIC THOMPSON

Brehtt drives home after a long day at the golf course. He does not stop to eat or have a beer. Straight home and goes to bed.

> *"Ah, great day. 36 holes on the golf course, 2,010 dollars in my pocket. I felt like Titanic Thompson out there and my hero and . . ."*
> *Z. . .Z. . . .Z. He is asleep and dreaming.*

The most famous gambler of all time whose real name was Alvin Clarence Thomas from Rogers, Arkansas. He learned many of his skills as a youngster.

Titanic traveled around the country, never staying too long in one place, as he did not want to become too familiar with people. Too much familiarity would wear out his welcome. If people knew of him and his phenomenal skills, he would not be able to make bets and get in card games.

He was skilled in cards, dice, golf, horseshoes, skeet, billiards, and proposition bets. He was the most womanizing, rake-hell, con man of all time. He would make unbelievable proposition bets that he set up to his advantage and win. One time, he passed a sign that said Joplin, 20 miles. He dug up the sign and replaced it five miles down the road towards Joplin. The next day he was returning from a fishing trip with friends and Titanic said that no way in hell was Joplin 20 miles away. The three friends argued until the two big gamblers put up 500 dollars that it was 20 miles. Using the odometer in the car, they measured the distance and it was 5 miles short of the 20-mile sign. Propositions like this one were good bets for Titanic as the odds were all in his favor.

Another time he beat a victim in pool and then offered him double or nothing that he could jump the pool table. The bet was taken and Titanic paced off a little distance, ran and dove over the table safely. One observer asked who the jumper was but no one knew. One observer said it should be Titanic because he is sinking everyone around here. The other story was that he got his name because he survived the sinking of the Titanic where he was into big card games. There may be more stories on the nickname. No one really knows. There are so many stories on Titanic that separating facts from folklore is difficult. However, the more preposterous the story, the more believable it becomes because he was so good.

All his plays were for him to win or he would not bet. For example, the checker champion of Missouri had a 10,000-dollar wager for anyone who could beat him. Taking no chances, Titanic did his preplanning. He wired the world's checker champion in Detroit to help him, not to teach him the game because he was not familiar with it, but to signal to him the moves. A peek hole was drilled in the ceiling above the game table. An electronic communication system was set up were the Detroit champion would peek through the hole and would signal to Titanic's leg with the mild electric shock for the correct move. Titanic quickly won, split the money with the Detroit guy, and went on his way. The Missouri guy was never the same after that.

He was the Arizona State trapshooting champion four consecutive years. It was said that he could throw a baseball from dead center field 400 feet to home plate without the aid of a bounce and he would challenge professional baseball players in throwing matches. One time, he challenged the horseshoe throwing world champion to a high stakes game and beat him out of $2,000.

Titanic was a genius in figuring out the odds on almost any situation, which is amazing because he had very little schooling. He spent most of his time hunting, fishing, poolroom playing, card playing and dice games. If you play the odds right your chances of winning are increased. In some of his proposition bets, the odds where 100 percent in his favor as he would set up the scam ahead of time. When the odds are in your favor, there is an advantage and a fair amount of safety in betting high.

Titanic spent so much time indoors in gambling establishments that he told Nick the Greek he needed to get outdoors for sun and fresh air, like in his days as a kid. Nick told him to take up golf but Titanic said there was not much point in the game. Nick then talked about getting out in broad daylight and beating some dude for a pocketful of money.

It never struck Titanic before so while driving home one day he stopped at a driving range. He talked to a man hitting balls and asked if he could hit a ball, as he had never done it before. He did and drove it to the 300-yard sign. The man gasped and said it was the longest drive he had ever seen. Titanic was now hooked. He then bought a driver and proceeded to his pool playing game.

When he got there he did his bragging routine that he could outdrive anyone in town. A set-up was made that one in three drives would go 300 yards which at that time was an extremely long distance. The golf balls and clubs were not as good then as they are now, so a 300-yard drive was worth seeing.

The pool hall emptied quickly to get to the driving range. Unfortunately, he lost the 500 dollar bet as it rained during the night and the field was wet. The ball had no roll when it landed so the drive was all carry, a good 285 with no roll.

Titanic paid the bet, and threw his golf club in the trashcan.

On recollection of his thought, he changed his mind, bought a set of golf clubs and practice balls. He spent time learning and practicing the game early in the mornings so there was less chance of being noticed.

Titanic set up his first proposition with a San Francisco golf pro after their poker game. Thompson said that golf was a kid's game and could not be too difficult. Naturally, the pro chided him about the difficulty of the game and he offered to play Titanic the next day so Titanic could see how difficult the game was. The pro wanted 10 dollars a hole and Titanic agreed.

Titanic was his usual brilliance in being all over the course looking for his ball and not finding it many times. The pro feeling sorry for him tried giving him some tips as they played. The pro won every hole and collected 90 dollars for the nine hole match.

That evening at the poker game Titanic got a ribbing with trash talking from the gang. Ti got mad and offered many excuses like that the pro was lucky and he had a bad day. Later in the game, the pro walks in and Titanic jumps him about his friends making fun of him so he wants another game with three strokes a hole for 1,000 dollars a hole. The pro will only give him two shots a hole and they will play 18 holes. The game is on the next morning. Titanic playing the crowd of poker players covered 30,000 dollars in bets.

The crowd showed up for tee time. Titanic hit his long and straight, 50 yards ahead of the pro. Titanic won every hole to give himself 56,000 dollars. He was now addicted to golf.

> *"In golf it does not matter so much how good you are but how good you make your bets. Do you give or take strokes and any other ground rules? Are the negotiation in your favor? In setting the rules of engagement, one must know the opponent. As Sam Snead said to never bet a stranger or anyone, unless you are positively sure of his true ability. Follow this rule and you will not likely be scammed - underestimate your ability and overestimate the ability of your opponent. Do not let ego override you. Unless you are sure, absolutely sure, walk away and don't let the trash talk get to you for walking away. You only bet when the odds and bets are in your favor, and not even. I will always remember Titanic's quote, "As I see it, the thing you gotta do is eliminate the risk beforehand; make sure you're gonna win before you put down a bet."*

He taught himself golf because it looked interesting, but the money involved with gambling bets was exceptional. Thousands of dollars were often laid on the line. He became so good that golf was one of his favorite means of finance. Hall of Fame golfer Ben Hogan called Titanic the best-shot maker he ever saw. "He can play right- or left-handed, you can't beat him". One hustle of his was to beat a golfer playing right-handed. After the match, he would offer the loser a chance to play again to get his money back. He would play left handed to give the loser a better chance of winning. Strange as it seems Titanic would win again. He was that good. Titanic even beat the famous Byron Nelson, a man who won eleven PGA golf tournaments in one year, by shooting a 29 on the back nine at Fort Worth's Ridglea Country Club. He beat Byron Nelson by one stroke.

I could not afford the cut in pay was Titanic's answer when people asked why he did not turn pro. Back then, professional golf tournaments did not have the money like today. Even the pros back then made a lot of the money with exhibitions and set-up matches with hotshots looking for action. Country clubs were ideal as the members had money and their interest in action to make big money with their hotshot golfers. Most of these set-up matches were for more money than winning a pro golf tournament.

In a high stakes poker game, Titanic left the game to go downstairs to the toilet. A rat ran across his feet, startled as he knocked over a crate in an attempt to regain balance. The crate fell on the rat and pinned him to the floor with only his head sticking out. The rat was still alive. The quick-witted Titanic is fast in seeing possible opportunities. He ran upstairs, sat down and complained how the place was infested with rats. He claimed he could go downstairs and shoot a rat within two minutes.

These poker players are gamblers on anything. They said it was impossible to be back in two minutes. So the routine begins with the betting game for 500 dollars and the ground rules of the clock is on and the rat has to be warm on arrival so that it is not some dead rat put away for such an opportunity.

The card game ceases and all is silent. Titanic rushes down the stairs, shoots the trapped rat, brings him up by the tail, collects his money and leaves.

Horseshoe pitching became popular after the war. Titanic saw this as a possible betting game for big money. He did a lot of practice and was able to throw about 80 out of 100 ringers. He was 80 percent efficient. He was ready and he went to Pittsburg where he would play bad so the next round could be played for more money. He hustled many of the players and made good money. As he ran out of competition, he started to look around for the world champion horseshoe pitcher by the name of Frank Jackson.

In time, Titanic found out that Jackson lived in Minneapolis. Titanic made contact and wanted a game. Jackson was ready so arrangements were made for a

$10,000 bet. Titanic got to Minneapolis and scouted the area. He found a wide alleyway between two buildings and built a horseshoe pit. He played the locals in order to build up his reputation as a highly skilled player. It is reported that Titanic hit 50 ringers in a row during a game in the alleyway. Word got around and Jackson is ready. Titanic was told of how good Jackson was and playing dumb, he gives the guy a 20-dollar bill to ask Jackson for a game.

Shortly, Jackson appears in the alleyway. He is quite confident, maybe arrogant as he says that if you are here to beat me you had better make it worth my while. The game is 10,000 dollars and 100 dollars side bets are made. A large crowd gathered. Most refused to bet against the world champion which they should have because Titanic wiped him clean as he threw ringers and most of Jackson's tosses where short. Titanic collected his winnings, apologized for his lucky day and quickly exited. Jackson was dejected, confused and humiliated.

Titanic had to get out of town quickly because he had the court set up a few feet long of regulation and he figured Jackson may soon figure it out.

> "This is surprising. A man with Jackson's experience should have figured something was amiss when most of his shots were short. Highly skilled athletes have excellent perceptions as to size, dimensions and distances. Basketball players have recognized if the basket was an inch too high or too low. It is hard to imagine but the folklore goes on."

In high stakes betting and gaming, Titanic was able to play and perform under pressure. The key to winning at high stakes is often just the ability to perform under pressure. Skeet shooting accuracy can be destroyed through pressure. The muscles tighten and the breathing becomes shorter, shallower and labored. One little flaw in the aim, shaking of the hand and arm, eyesight, and timing will miss the target. Titanic was the skeet-shooting champion of Arizona for four years running. In golf, the same reaction to pressure is required. Sinking a three-foot putt is easy but with thousands of dollars on the line, the putt seems like 60 feet if the pressure is not controlled.

"So true. I damn near missed a four footer when I started to think of the money on this putt. Thinking of the money before the putt is getting ahead of yourself when your focus is on the money and the putt has not been made.

I remember the true story of Tommy Armour being paired with Johnny Revolta in a PGA pro golf tournament. Revolta was near the lead in the closing holes with a four-foot putt. He left the putt short. A man in the gallery yelled "Gutless".

Armour walked over to the crowd and callenged the man with a bet for 5,000 dollars if he could make the same putt. The man told Armour not to be ridiculous and he accepted the challenge that right after the tournament ended he would try the putt for 5,000 dollars.

The ball was placed on the same spot. A large gallery formed around the green. As the man addressed the ball, he started to sweat. His hands began to shake. He backed away and tried to compose himself. He finally takes the putt – short and wide of the hole. The man, being a gentleman, apologized to Revolta and said that when he got over the ball, he couldn't even see the hole. I had no idea of what pressure can do to you. Armour told the guy that the bet was off and to take his money. Back then 5,000 in the 1930s was a lot of money."

Bowling was not out of the question for Titanic. His athletic skills naturally helped him as he found the bowling alleys good for gambling just like in golf. At one alley, he found that the duckpin record has stood for 30 years. Titanic bet the owner he could break the record within ten games. Word got around and soon 5,000 was on the table. Titanic broke the record in the third game.

Sometimes despite immaculate preparations, things go bad with lady luck. Titanic and his wife were vacationing in Tijuana, Mexico. Needing a little action, he used his money to fix a race with the jockeys. The odds were 8 to 1 so he called bookmakers in various cities for a total of 100,000 dollars.

The race started well and their horse was working his way into the lead. Down the stretch, he was well ahead by 100 yards, a sizeable lead. The crowd was yelling and screaming. Excitement was high. Then 30 yards from the finish line, a deathly silence lowered. The horse collapsed from a broken leg.

> *"Sometimes planning and preparation are not enough. Luck, good and bad, may determine the future."*

One time Titanic walked into a bar because it had a pool table. Two big old boys, over six feet and 250 pounds, chided him for not taking a drink. Finally, Titanic had enough. He asked the boys how strong they were and naturally they bragged. They laughed as they thought the test of strength would be against the skinny Titanic. He bet them that neither one of them could carry a brick in his hand for five miles and then drop it on the bar. The brothers could only come up with 20 dollars so the bet was made. They took one of the brothers five miles down the road and dropped him off.

In time, the person arrived with the brick, walked up to the bar cocky as hell but the big grin soon left his face. He tried to lift his arm to the level of the bar so he could drop the brick on the bar. He couldn't. His finger muscles were so constricted the brick dropped to the floor. Titanic took the money and left. The brothers, disappointed, wanted another drink but also had to leave – they had no money.

Titanic was not only famous, but he often hung around with other famous people, even legends. He and Nick the Greek, another famous gambler, often worked together. Minnesota Fats of pool hall fame called Titanic the greatest action man of all time. He was often seen with movie stars and sport heroes. He was also linked with Myrna Loy and Jean Harlow of silver screen fame. Houdini even tried to follow him to find his secrets. Titanic was so gutsy that he cheated on a bet with Al Capone and still lived.

Divorce rates are high with a man who is always travelling away from his wife. As a ladies' man, he could just as easily talk a woman into loving him as he could talk a man into a bet. There was something about him people thought they could tame. He counted on that underestimation and used it frequently. Titanic married five times and all of them teenagers. When he died at the age of 81, his last wife of 19 years was 37. This guy was something else.

> *"Titanic was a womanizer so why did he get married anyway? He always had women; he travelled with women. Why get married? He must have known that women would leave him as he was rarely at home. He was my kind of guy."*

In his younger years, he was honing his skills. He would toss pennies in a small box 20 feet way. He would do the same in tossing cards into a hat. One of his first jobs on leaving home when 16 years old was with a snake oil salesman who was also a champion rifle marksman who would demonstrate hitting pie plates thrown in the air. Titanic got a job with him when he showed how he could hit a pie plate six times when thrown in the air. After a while, Titanic took a solid washer and told the snake oil man he could shoot a hole in it. He threw the washer in the air, it came down nearby, and it was checked. Sure enough, there was a hole in it. Titanic said that this would be better than shooting pie plates. The snake oil man said it would and Titanic then explained the trick. He showed the solid washer, then palmed it and threw up a washer with a hole already in it.

> *"So simple. So effective. The simplicity of it all fools the people."*

As for his card playing, Titanic was legendary. He could palm, shift, anything with the cards. He was considered the best. His fast, smooth talk always seemed to increase the bets when he needed it. His winnings were often invested in oil and land. He was well off.

> *"It's raining, blowing and kinda cold so I am going to stay at home and read about famous golf scams or bets. Most bets are scams as one negotiates the bets to his advantage. When a person negotiates a bet to his advantage then he is conning or defrauding the other person."*

Brehtt does not even get dressed. He just sits and reads, spaced with a few giggles, laughs and wows every so often. As he reads:

Bing Crosby was a serious golfer who hated to pay off his debts. Even Bob Hope had a hard time collecting from Bing. Anyway, Bing was playing LaVerne Moore, the 'Mysterious John Montague,' a big time hustler. Montague said he could beat Bing using a bat, shovel and a rake. On the first hole, Bing was on the green in two and two putted for a four. Montague hit the ball twice with the bat. He was in the bunker lying two so he scraped it out of the bunker with the shovel and used the rake as a pool cue to get his par. Bing just walked off and went to the bar. He was finished with Montague.

John Montague was a man of many talents. He could step on his ball in a sand trap and blast it out with a two wood. He could take a five iron and hit two balls at once, one ball would go right, and the other would go left. He would have a caddie lie down with a kitchen match sticking out of his mouth and Montague would take a full swing with a 2-iron and light the match.

At the Lakeside golf course, famous for celebrities, he would have someone lift the window and use a drinking glass to keep it open and he would chip balls through the open window and never miss. The glass varied from a cocktail glass to even a shot glass. This guy was another Titanic Thompson.

One-time birds were sitting, in line, on a wire. Montague said he could hit the bird on the right. The bird was 175 yards away. He did. This story became folklore. Each telling became more grandiose and the bird became smaller and the distance longer.

Montague had the name 'mysterious' tagged on to him. Nobody knew him, where he came from or any of his past. He was a mystery to everyone. However, this is not unusual as this is what con artists strive for. It is hard to get a bet or make a scam if people know you and your abilities. The great ones like Titanic also played this way. Here we have a phenomenon in the con world – they all have nicknames.

The worlds of Titanic and Montague were very similar. In fact, some of the stories would be mixed up as to who did what. Folklore over time does this.

Golfers who would play with Montague for big money even as they knew they were going to lose. They just wanted in on the action. It was almost as if they would become famous by associating with Montague because he was famous. They paid for this false belief by losing bets to Montague.

Not all big bets are played by good golfers. Sometimes poor golfers make big bets. The movie director Henry King was to play the famous actor Adolph Menjou for the eighth flight championship. The match was scheduled and rescheduled as each was ducking the other. Finally it was played. Menjou won on the 18th hole to a large gallery with lots of betting. Neither golfer shot under 120.

Sometimes the con or scam is not used. Deception is the key. Deception fools the opposition and he makes his own mistakes. Although this has happened many times, it was a valuable lesson to Sam Snead. He and his opponent came to a long par 3 and Sam did not know what club to hit. Out of the corner of his eye he saw his opponent pull out a fairway wood and tuck it under his arm waiting for Sam to hit. Sam took out his 2-iron and hit the shot. The ball sailed over the green. The opponent put the wood back in his bag and pulled out another club.

Dutch Harrison, a PGA tour player, would send his caddy to the caddy yard prior to a tournament. Dutch would get his game and money match ready and then would ask if he could take one of the caddies as his partner. He would then point to his shill and off they go. The shill played only as good as needed to collect the money. He was so good that his name was Herman Keiser, the 1946 Master's Golf Champion.

Another deception was with Doug Sanders of PGA fame. Dr. Cary Middlecoff had an exceptional caddy who was amazing at judging distance by eyesight. There were no GPS systems for golf then. Sanders paid a course worker to cut some pins to make them shorter and add some of the cuts to make the others longer. Poor Middlecoff was short or long all day. His caddie's distances were slightly off but often enough for disastrous results. Twenty years later the caddie found out the truth.

A sports writer bet Sam Snead 1,000 dollars that he could not take 18 putts or less for a round of golf. Sam goes out, misses every green, and chips up for a one putt. One time he chipped in. After nine holes, the sports writer and Sam settled the bet for 500 dollars.

After all this heavy reading Brehtt falls asleep.

Brehtt wakes up from his dream.

> "Today is practice day. I must be able to be perfect in any con or bet I make."

Brehtt clears the table and gets to work. He pulls out his books and articles for reinforcement of prior knowledge. He also studies to provide a twist in some of his bets in case the old scam is recognized. Only the good, no, only the exceptional, survive.

Brehtt takes a match and lights it. The trick is to see if the match can be held upside down for twenty seconds. The trick is to hold the match upside down but move it slowly from side to side so the flame misses the fingers.

Brehtt takes a full sheet of a newspaper like the one he just read and tries to fold it in half eight times. It cannot be done.

Brehtt puts his two palms together and then bends the two middle fingers over each other so they rest on the knuckle of the opposite hand. Place a coin between the tips of the two ring fingers. Separate the two fingers holding the coin. It can't be done.

Next, he slides a match between the ring, middle and index finger so that the match rests on the top of the ring and index finger but underneath the middle finger. Now try to break the match with the fingers and arm remaining straight. It can't be done. To do it, hit the palm against the table and the match will break.

Be careful with this one. Have a person stand with his back to a wall and his heels touching the baseboard. Place a bill, one, five or whatever the bet if he or she can pick it up without falling. They can't.

This one, even though people know this one, they are still fascinated by it. If there are over 30 people in a room, the odds are that two will have the same birthday. Have the people call out their birthdays and before the 30th person calls someone will have the same birthday as someone else.

Brehtt then returned to his other skills in cards, dice, three card monte, tossing pennies and throwing playing cards into a hat.

> *"The key to my efficiency is on smoothness of executing my skill. I must practice. Lots of practice."*

WOMEN IN THE TRADE

Brehtt finishes a day of practice. He watches the news and then reads his con book on women con artists.

Not all con artists were men. Women were involved and are good. Women had two assets that could turn a man to murder. They are beauty and sex. They may not get the sex but the sex is a possibility in the man's eye. Often, she is only interested in the money. To her, sex is an illusion she creates in the man's eye. However, if the scam is big and rewarding enough, sex will take place.

Men have the illusion that women are helpless and not as smart as they are. Put an attractive woman on the golf driving range and invariably men will approach and offer her tips, even though such men may not even be able to break 100. Oh, the ego.

Many women are not hard-core con artists but they do a soft-con like pressure into marriage, I need a new dress, or car. Here the women use the men's urges for sex to get the desired object or money. Sometimes the con is about pregnancy for marriage or abortion money. The male con artists greatly outnumber the female artists and no one seems to know why. If we add the number of soft-cons women use daily the statistics may change.

How about Chessie Chadwick? She was able to pass herself off as the illegitimate daughter of Andrew Carnegie, the richest bachelor in the world. She was believable as banks and millionaires lent her lots of money, estimated over 20 million. Many business, financial institutions and leaders of business and industry were ruined by her. She was arrested lying in bed with a money belt around her containing 100,000 dollars.

Chadwick starts using forgery to build a bank account. She was arrested and when released, left Canada. Her next con was that she was Andrew Carnegie's illegitimate daughter and Carnegie was paying her big money to keep it quiet. It worked because no one wanted to embarrass Carnegie. Over eight years she amassed 20 million dollars in forged bank notes. Eventually she was arrested and sent to prison. The Citizen's National Bank of Oberlin was forced into bankruptcy after it loaned Chadwick $800,000.

This guy had balls. He was not a women but he set himself up as a doctor for women. He was a sewer worker that passed himself off as a gynecologist. He told women that he could diagnose their health problems by studying photos and that sexual intercourse was the cure. In time, he was arrested for multi counts of rape, and procuring unlawful sexual acts. His victims ranged from 13 to 21 years old.

Susanna Mildred Hill was a con artist with potential suitors. She was 60 years old and her scam was with 'pen pals'. No internet back then, but the pen pal system worked very well for her. She did well with gifts and money rolling in from the pen pals. This was the beginning of the lonely-hearts club scams.

Sylvia Browne, born Sylvia Celeste Shoemaker, was an author who claims to have psychic and spiritual medium powers. It seems most con artists go by an assumed name. She was hosted on many popular TV shows and had her own hour-long show on Radio, discussing paranormal issues and giving callers advice. In 1992, Browne was convicted of investment fraud and grand theft. Her claims and predictions were not coming true. She was investigated and charged.

Mary Peck Butterworth was a counterfeiter in colonial America. Mary Butterworth allegedly started her counterfeiting operation around 1716. Butterworth has an interesting procedure in counterfeiting. She used starched cotton cloths to produce counterfeit bills, rather than the metal plates used more commonly in counterfeiting. Using a slightly dampened piece of starched cloth, she was able to lift ink from a genuine bill. With a hot iron, she transferred a pattern from the cloth to a blank paper bill, and then inked the pattern by hand with quill pens. The original cotton cloth was easily disposed of through burning, leaving no evidence of a crime.

Butterworth allegedly organized her counterfeiting with the entire family. She sold the bills at 100 percent profit.

Ultimately, the court dismissed all charges against her for lack of hard evidence.

Charlene Corley is a former defense contractor who was convicted in 2007 on two counts of conspiracy. Over the course of nine years leading up to September 2006, the company owned by Corley and her sister received over 20 million dollars from the United States Department of Defense for fraudulent shipping costs. One example of many was being paid $998,798 for shipping two 19-cent washers. In 2009, Corley was sentenced to six years in prison and ordered to pay $15.5 million in restitution.

The Department of Defense had 112 fraudulent invoices, totaling 20.5 million dollars in illegitimate charges, for parts sent to priority military installations, including destinations in Iraq and Afghanistan. More examples of the fraud are: $445,640 for shipping an $8.75 elbow pipe. $492,096 for shipping a $10.99 machine thread plug. $403,436 for shipping six machine screws worth a total of $59.94.

Sheila Ann Dixon was the forty-eighth mayor of Baltimore, Maryland. On January 9, 2009, Dixon was indicted on twelve felony and misdemeanor counts, including perjury, theft, and misconduct. She misappropriated gift cards intended for the poor. She resigned as part of the plea bargain.

Debra Harrison was a Lieutenant Colonel in the U.S. Army Reserve who served in the Coalition Provisional Authority from 2003 to 2004. She was arrested on December 15, 2005 on charges involving bribery, money laundering and fraud. Harrison allegedly stole between $80,000 and $100,000 in funds from the U.S. governing administration in Iraq, using the money to install a deck and hot tub in her New Jersey home. She pleaded guilty and was sentenced in June 2009 to 30 months in prison.

Antoinette Millard was an impostor who used the name Lisa Walker when she pretended to be a Saudi princess. In May 2004, she claimed she was a Saudi Arabian princess and that she that she was mugged and the robbers had stolen insured jewelry worth $262,000.

Millard joined the New York City high society with claims of being a lawyer, graduate of Boston University, a model for Victoria's Secret or Bergdorf Goodman or Brown Brothers Harriman vice-president. She also expected a 7 million dollar divorce settlement.

Eventually the bubble burst. Millard was charged with insurance fraud, attempted grand larceny and forgery. She was released on bail worth $100,000 but faced 15 years in jail if convicted.

On August 2, 2005, she pled guilty to grand larceny and insurance fraud. She claimed that she had been obviously mentally incompetent when she had opened her credit account and that the credit card company should have realized that and not issued her the card. She claimed symptoms of anorexia, depression, anxiety attacks and that she had a head tumor and sued for million dollars. Her reasoning led to a sentence of a year in mental institution for treatment.

"I guess her plea bargain got what she needed."

Laura Pendergest-Holt was a Ponzi scheme artist, a financier, and former Chief Investment Officer of Stanford Financial Group. In 2009, Stanford Financial became the subject of several fraud investigations, and on February 17, 2009, Pendergest-Holt was charged by the U.S. Securities and Exchange Commission with fraud and multiple violations of U.S. securities laws for massive ongoing fraud involving $8 billion in certificates of deposits. It was a massive Ponzi scheme. Holt was sentenced to three years in prison, followed by three years of supervised probation.

Esther Elizabeth Reed was an American convicted on fraud and identity theft. She took on several identities. At various times, she claimed to be a skilled chess player, and claimed chess tournaments were her income to friends to cover up her financial scams.

Reed assumed the identity of Natalie Bowman to attend Harvard University. At Harvard, Reed joined the debating team. She was investigated for espionage, as she was romantic with West Point cadets.

She was so notorious that she made the 10-most-wanted fugitive list and America's Most Wanted list. She finally confessed, pleaded guilty, got 51 months in prison, instead of a possible 47 years in prison.

Ashley Todd was a volunteer for John McCain's bid for the presidency of America. She claimed to be assaulted by a Barack Obama supporter. She was charged with fraud and served probation. The timing, two weeks before the election, may have been to discredit the Obama campaign.

Brehtt is now tired, between awake and asleep.

> "Ahhhh, these women. They're gutsy. I wonder what it would be like married to one of them? Zzzzzz. . . ."

CHAPTER 18

The SPY LADY

On entering her apartment, the spy lady is still in turmoil. She feels a little dizzy. She walks to her bedroom to change clothes but never makes it. She falls over on the floor.

The next morning a phone call. "Natasha, Stella here, I tried to reach you last night. I phoned several times but no answer. Are you okay?"

"Yep, I'm okay. I guess I conked out and fell asleep so good. I never heard the phone. Sorry. What's up?"

"Are you up to going 'there' tonight?"

"Yeah sounds good. I'll pick you up at 730. It's a little earlier than usual but it'll give us a good start and we can pull a few trains together."

"You are so nasty. I love it."

THE CON MAN

Brehtt wakes up, eats and mopes around the house.

> *"I need something different today. Too many days are the same. . .*
> *What could I do to change the routine. . .*

After a half hour it hits him.

> *"Hey, how about some blackjack at the Casinos? I haven't done that*
> *in a long time. Yeahhhh. . .*

He gets up from the breakfast table and goes to his library and pulls out his books on blackjack, opens them and starts to study. Actually, he knows the procedure; he just needs to brush up on the memorization of the tables.

> *"This is one game where mistakes are costly, so he starts from the*
> *beginning with all the details covered. By knowing everything*
> *perfectly, confidence is created. The mind must not be touched or*
> *plagued with doubt. There must be no hesitation or uncertainty in*
> *making a play or bet. Precision play. Precise play. Accurate play."*

Brehtt lies on the floor with his books in front of him. His first move is to study the charts on what to do with the cards in your hand and the dealer's cards.

> *If I have 8 and the dealer's card showing is 2 to an ace then hit.*

> *If I have 9 and the dealer's card is a 2 then hit.*

> *If I have 9 and the dealer's card is a 3 to 6 then double down.*

> *If I have 9 and the dealer's card is a 7 to ace then hit.*

> *If I have 10 and the dealer's card is a 2 to 9 then double down.*

> *If I have 10 and the dealer's card is a 10 or ace then hit.*

If I have a . . . . .

He studies the chart for an hour and keeps testing himself to make sure it is down perfect. Every possible combination of card between dealer and player is studied. He reinforces in his mind combinations for a hit (take a card), stand (no more cards), double down (double the bet on the first two cards), and split (two similar cards can be split and played as two hands).

Now that he is back in form with the playing procedures. He moves on to card counting. Card counting is when the player counts or gives a value to each card played. The values are: cards 2 to 6 get a +1 value. Cards 7 to 9 get a zero value. Cards 10, face cards, and ace get a - value. For example, card 6 (+1), card 4 (+1), card 8 (0), card ace (-1) for a total of +1.

As the cards turn up, the total will reveal who has the advantage. If the total count is a minus, you bet less because there are more low cards in the deck. You bet less because the overall percentage favors the dealer. If the count is a plus the player has the advantage. The higher the plus count the more the advantage goes to the player. There are different counting systems but they all are basically the same in indicating the cards left in the deck as high or low cards.

To do this under game conditions takes skill and lots of practice. The cards flip so fast it can be difficult to maintain the count. The dealers play fast for this reason. They do not want you to think and analyze the situation. They want your money fast.

Brehtt takes out a deck and flips each card, face side up, as fast as he can. He makes the count as he speeds along.

> *"This is easy, but it will not be this easy in the casino. Things move fast and there are plenty of distractions. Concentration and focus are the utmost requirements."*

He has done this before so he is just reinforcing his past. Past learning is coming back. The old riding a bicycle theory of you never forget how to ride a bicycle. Talent is never lost, it is just misplaced. His talent is there so he just practices it a little and he is back in form.

Brehtt now reviews his money management system, which is not too difficult. The basic money management is in the card counting. Minus count, bet low. Plus count bet high. The higher the minus count, lower the bet. The higher the plus count, higher the bet. This is simple, but the real problem is betting high and low is a tip-off to the dealer and the pit boss. The betting has to be disguised, so one has to make some mistakes so the routine is not too noticeable. The trick is to play like a 'rube', a 'hick', or a beginner with beginner's luck in just hitting the big payoffs. One must realize that the dealer and the pit boss are not dummies.

One of the best money management strategies is not to get greedy. Win some money and walk away. Live to come back another day. Win too much money at once and you may well be met at the door and not invited to return. Casinos are not charitable businesses. They are there for one purpose only – to take your money. If you win too much, violence has been known to occur. Casinos are very protective of their money.

Blackjack dealers used to play with one deck. This made card counting easy. This was hurting their business so they went to two decks and finally had to go to four and then six decks. This made the counting more difficult but not impossible. Brilliant minds were still able to do the counting and win. The casinos did the next thing to keep their money by barring card counters, not letting them in. The casinos worked together with photos of the card counters and shared them among each other. The few top counters then took to disguises but soon had trouble with that. Beat the casino – almost impossible.

Brehtt practices all day, goes to bed early, reads his con games history books and falls asleep.

"A good day. I feel good. A day after a good day of blackjack practice. I feel lucky. Oh, shit. Blackjack is not luck. I practice to

beat luck. Sometimes luck happens and I take it but I never rely on luck. If a con depends on luck, I must walk away from it. Depending on luck often results in things going bad and a mark may get pissed and shoot me, beat me, or have someone else do it. The key to the con or any skill is talent. If I don't have it, I will develop it with practice and lots of practice. If I lack the talent then I will drop the con from my repertoire. Like Titanic Thompson said, make a bet only if you are sure of winning."

He eats, dresses and drives off to the casino. It's a 75-minute drive so he plays the game in his head, a pregame warm-up. He parks the car and enters the casino. Like always, the lights are flashing, the sounds are echoing, and beautiful women in scanty clothes are running around delivering drinks. All this is designed for distraction of the players.

The drinks are free or cost very little. The casino knows that what they give away in free drinks they will get back with drunk or semi-drunk players overspending.

Overspending is a big problem. For some reason gamblers think the next bet is salvation, the big score. They cannot think to cut the losses and get out.

Brehtt walks around looking at the different games in the casino, but keeping an eye on the blackjack tables. He will not sit down until the dealer is near the end of the shoe (the card holder to deal from). If he sits down at the middle of the shoe dealing his count will not be accurate as he does not know the count when the shoe started its action.

Soon he finds a table, sits down and plays a few hands before the shuffle of the cards. He returns the dealer's greetings. He gets his 5-dollar chips and bets.

He bets two chips, ten dollars, his two cards are both aces, the dealer shows a 10. Wow, good way to start. This is not luck, it is coincidence. He splits. Always split aces. The dealer busts, as his hand is a five and then an 8. Brehtt is off to a good start.

The game is rolling along and Brehtt is managing to stay a little over even.

"At least I am not losing. Maybe time to run it."

He increases his betting, slowly to avoid suspicion. Two hours later, he is up 650 dollars. He gets up and walks away. He goes to the dining area. Casinos have good food at a very reasonable price. Some places the price is very low. Good food, low price and cheap drinks keeps the gamblers there. In fact, some people go in, eat, and go out, never playing a game.

After an hour break, he goes to the crap table, takes a few small bets and leaves for the blackjack table. He returns to a different table, the 10-dollar chip table. He follows his same routine. Easy small bets. Suddenly, the count is high in his favor. He drops a few chips, ten of them and hits the win. He is up to almost two thousand dollars. The dealer is watching him and it looks like he signaled the pit boss.

Brehtt picks up his chips and walks toward the cashier's window. The pit boss accompanies him.

"Your lucky day, mister."

"Yeah, never this lucky."

"You must come back again . . . but you better not be this lucky again."

"Jesus Christ, is this a threat? He should keep his mouth shut because I will be back in disguise and really hit you guys."

He cashes in and leaves – happy as hell as he goes home. Gets ready for bed and lounges as he reads about Zen mystics and how they control their body's heartbeat, feelings to cold and heat, their calmness, food consumption, their breathing, etc. It is amazing.

"I'm going to try this."

He lies down facing the large-hand clock on the wall with a large second hand. He holds his hands on his stomach with the right hand taking the pulse off the left hand. He takes the pulse for 30 seconds and then doubles it for the minute count. He rests for a few minutes for the body to adjust to the prone position. Just going from standing to lying should lower the beat. After the rest, he is now at 68 beats per minute.

He concentrates on the beat, relaxes the body and he is able to get down to 62. This is good but he is overconfident and it goes up to 67. Back to deep thought in imagining he is a Zen monk, sitting on the mountaintop, in the snow, in short pants. He also adjusts his breathing to make sure it is slow, deep and steady. In 20 minutes, he is down to 55 beats and holding.

"I want to get into the 40s. So far I'm not making it. I need more practice.

Brehtt keeps practicing. He goes out for lunch and buys a heart rate monitor and breathing monitor. He bypasses supper as he is practicing his body control. He is down to 52 but cannot get under 50 beats per minute. His deep breathing is down to four and one-half breaths per minute.

"I am not giving up. I will get it."

He practices until bedtime where he reads his book from Amazon that came in today's mail. The book is about spies in the C.I.A. (America Intelligence), the K.G.B. (Soviet Union Intelligence) and the MI6 (British Intelligence).

He is reading along until he comes to the second chapter on lying. He is interested in this because cons are about lying. The polygraphs (lie detector) really grabbed his attention as the polygraph does not measure lies; it measures body response to questions. The body response to a question is then used to determine if the body response indicates lie or the truth.

"If a person can control his body's response to the question he can then control the polygraph machine and make a lie the truth. If I can get this lower heart rate and breathing, I can beat the polygraph.

This is interesting. A psychotic and/or a sociopath will beat the polygraph because they have no remorse or feelings. The body response does not convey their feelings. They can kill and their body response will not give them away."

A polygraph is a device that attaches electrodes to your body to record heart rate, blood pressure, respiration rate, galvanic skin response. Usually, the first question is your name and the machine registers your responses. A series of easy questions like, age, address, job, etc. are to further your basic responses. Then the question may be did you kill so and so. If you did kill the person then your body is supposed to feel guilty and respond by heart rate going up, increased breathing and sweating from the galvanic skin response. If you did not kill the person then your response should remain normal. Now the tricky part is that you may not have killed the person you may panic because you are afraid they may think so anyway or you may feel they will not believe you. Such thoughts may well make your responses higher than normal.

Many factors are taken into account with the lie detector. The results depend on how good and experienced the tester is. How good is the reliability of the machine or the machine and tester together? It is something like 30 to 40 percent reliable. Because the unreliability is so high, some states will not allow it in the courtroom. A wise decision.

Evidently, you cannot be forced to take a lie detector test. The unfortunate side is that people think that a refusal to take the test is an admission of guilt. If in such a position and you refuse make sure you state why you refuse. Polygraphs are not accurate enough to be reliable.

The machine can be beat. Psychopaths and sociopaths beat the machine all the time. Evidently, there are four types of lies. Prosocial lies are lies that help other people out. Self-enhancement lies make yourself look good but do not hurt others. Selfish lies help you and hurt others. Antisocial lies are deliberate lies to hurt other people.

To beat the test, learn how to control your physiological responses of the heart, blood pressure, breathing, sweating, etc. Spies learn these techniques. Do not panic or let anxiety show? The test administrator will be very polite, accommodating and friendly in an effort to get you to relax. If you can't relax and panic in your responses will not be normal, if so, the tester better be exceptionally good, which few are? Do not be talkative even if you are nervous. Just answer with a yes or no.

People under stress start to breathe fast and shallow. Slow down the breathing and breathe deeply and steadily. Some responders to the lie detector test will throw things off by pinching themselves, digging fingernails in the skin, anything to cause pain to the body and in turn cause a physiological response and a lack of consistency in your responses to the machine.

If you have a chance apply antiperspirant to your body and fingertips to keep you dry. Staying dry messes the galvanic skin response as sweat is needed for its measurement of stress. Sweat absorbing body powder will also work but it may well be too noticeable to the tester.

Some have used beta-blockers to help calm themselves down for the test but if they do a drug test prior to the polygraph you are done. Melatonin may also work as it is taken to help people sleep. Sam-e (S-adenosyl- methionine) an over the counter supplement may also work.

Mentally, one must not let the authority, testers, police, etc. intimidate you. Ignore them and be confident in your answers.

> "Ahh, this is interesting. The first person to create a lie detector used only the blood pressure response to the questions. This was the forerunner, which became more complete with time. This person, William Marston was a psychologist and teacher but he also created the comic strip Wonder Woman. He lived with two women in a ménage-et-trois. This may have helped in his sexual fantasies and feminism. This was back in 1914 and was uncommon then. Wonder Woman is still popular today as is his lie detector, which is now known as the polygraph machine because of the many responses it now measures."

Let's look at the validity of the polygraph. The Green River killings in Oregon were committed by the serial killer Gary Ridgway. He was given the polygraph, he passed it, and so he gets released. Once released he continues his killings. The reason for him passing the test seems to be that he was a psychopath. He has no emotions for his behavior and so the polygraph did not register.

In 1982, Melvin Foster, a murder suspect, failed the polygraph. He was convicted but later DNA evidence found Foster not guilty. Foster had a nervous tic and this may well have led to the failing of the polygraph. The polygraph naturally registered the body's response from the tics. A good tester should have recognized the tic and nullified the test.

Here is a little conflict. Wen Ho Lee a Chinese-American nuclear scientist was suspected of selling nuclear secrets to the Chinese. The U.S. Department of Energy said he was ok, as he passed the test. The FBI got involved and said he failed the tests. A royal mix-up. He went to jail, later was released and then the government had to pay him 1.65 million in damages.

CHAPTER 19

THE LADY SPY

Natasha and Stella are lying on their back slowly coming down from their sexual high. They turn and look at each other and smile. They say nothing. They are done. Neither could remember how many men and women. They took on all comers. They are now tired and worn out. Besides, what can they say? As they gaze at each other, their eyes say it all. For Natasha her head is cleared and she feels better. In the span of five hours, she was able to forget her assassination plans. For Stella it was a good romp in the hay.

In their familiar routine, they wobble around looking for their clothes. Their lovers could produce no more and were gone. On finding their clothes, they dressed and went home.

THE CON MAN

Brehtt raises the bet, "If I sink this putt, I'll put $500 for you guys to cover.

> *"I know this putt because two days ago I spent the evening when the course was closed practicing this putt. In fact, I hit my approach here to set up the putt."*

"You're on, scum bag," yells Tommy. "The odds on sinking a 45 foot putt are less than 3 percent. Since you are dumber than hell, I am going to double your bet, 1,000 dollars says you do not make it. USGA golf rules apply. No tricks or word play. He must hit the ball and it goes in or out with no devises or anything to help the ball."

The other three players put their money down.

"Fair enough. I have no intentions in deceiving you guys. I just wanted to show you true ability."

"Shut-up and hit the fucking ball."

Brehtt walks to the ball, looks around studying the terrain and slopes, grain, etc. He then walks around to the hole and studies the line from the hole to the ball. He then walks along the side of the line carefully studying everything. He returns to behind the ball, studies the line, proceeds to the ball, and takes his stance.

> *"I put on a good show. There was no need for it but it does add a little drama. I know this putt from all the practice. The putt does not break as it looks. It is one of those deceptive illusions. All golfers have experienced it. My practice knows this."*

When his body is in position, he looks at the hole, down at the ball and strokes it.

The ball takes off. The guys laugh.

"That is the worst line to the hole. You're going to miss."

The laughing slows down and stops. The ball turns slightly to the hole, slowly inching along, slow enough for the golfers to feel sick with disbelief. Slowly the ball nears the hole. The golfers are transfixed, cannot move, hypnotized by the ball.

"Clank, rattle, and the ball falls in."

The money is collected and they walk into the clubhouse to eat and play poker.

The game starts with the four of them and soon, 5 others join in.

Like most poker games, Brehtt was doing all right. He had a nice pile of chips. As the game went on late into the night, the players were getting a little inebriated. Alcohol and fatigue takes its toll in reasoning and thinking clearly.

"You fucking cheater. You took me for $500 in skins and $1000 in a putt and now your money pot is a little too high for an honest man."

Tommy jumps up and pulls a small pistol, aims at Brehtt, and shoots.

Brehtt is on the floor. The guys crowd around to check him.

"I'm alright."

Everyone is in shock. Nothing like this has ever happened.

> "Holy fuck. This is surreal. This is one time I knew how to dodge a bullet. The trick is to not watch the gun or the hand of the shooter. Watch the shooter's eyes. Just prior to the pull of the trigger, the eyes will take a squint effect which is natural when a loud noise is coming. The squint precedes the trigger pull. See the squint then fall down. Just get out of the way of the line of the shot, quickly, very quick."

Brehtt gets up and goes for Tommy but stops. Tommy is in a daze, paralyzed, confused. He cannot believe what he just did. Everyone is looking at Tommy.

Sirens are coming. It is too late to escape. Tommy was the first out but was caught by the police. Amazingly, the police covered all doors. No one got out.

All card players were arrested and taken to police headquarters and thrown in jail for the night.

The next morning preliminary interrogations began.

"Ah, shit," the chief bemoaned. "Give them all the polygraph test. They all took the test because they all knew they were not guilty."

> *Brehtt knew otherwise. He knew who the card cheater was. It was Bert, the guy with the second largest pile of chips. Tommy attempted to shoot the wrong guy. Fatigue and alcohol played its role. I knew who the cheat was because he kept using his fingernails to indent the edges of the cards. When such cards came to me, I would press the edges so that the indent would get filled again and be unnoticeable. I was making sure of the procedure before saying anything but Tommy took action before I could do or say anything. I was going to call the game and tell the players if they could identify the cards lying face down on the table. I would name the cards and then show them how it was done. This is going to be interesting."*

It's Brehtt's turn. He goes into the testing room where a friendly man in a business suit greets him. The testers, if they are police do not wear their uniform, as it may be intimidating to the person being tested. The tester uses pleasantries to try to relax the testee, but it is no surprise to Brehtt. He has studied all this.

He is hooked up and the first question is out.

"Is your name Brehtt Bennett?"

"Yes."

"Where you playing cards at the Country Club last night?"

"Yes."

"Do you play golf?"

"Yes."

"Do you play for money when golfing?"

"Yes."

"Do you cheat at cards or golf?"

"No."

> *"Sometimes I have cheated but only to get back at another cheater. I never cheat in an honest game. Brehtt starts working his physiological responses."*

"Never, ever or sometimes."

"Never."

"Why not?"

"I am good enough to not have too."

"Did you cheat on that 45 foot putt yesterday?"

"Didn't have to."

> *"I practiced that putt. Start deep breathing slowly and deeply. Slow down the heart rate and blood pressure. I practiced this and I can do it. I can't let this idiot think my practice was cheating.*

"Why did Tommy shoot at you?"

"Because I had the most money and he was mad at me because he lost the putting bet."

"Do you know who was cheating?"

"No."

> "Brehtt works a little harder with his concentration on his physiological responses. Occasionally he would pinch his leg or finger."

"Well, Mr. Bennett that will be all."

A half hour later, the tester and the chief talk to Brehtt and tell him that he passed the test with flying colors. The chief looks at Brehtt, "Brehtt, you've been around. You are good at what you do and I know all your bets are legitimate. Off the record, do you know who was cheating?"

"Yes. . ."

"You're lying," yells the tester. The polygraph said you did not know who was cheating."

"Yeah, that piece of shit you call a polygraph only measures body response. It cannot measure lies and truths. It is your interpretation that makes it a lie or a truth. Psychopaths, sociopaths, and people like me who train our body responses can beat the machine.

"I should have known," laughs the chief. "Tommy will have to be charged, and no one was hurt, so that is one good thing. What about the cheater?"

"Don't worry chief, we will fix him in due time. He will be milked so bad that even your charges and arrests could never hurt him like we can."

"Yeah, I'll buy that. See you Brehtt."

"Chief, how about a golf game?"

"Brehtt, get the fuck out of here," as he laughs and rolls his eyes.

WHY DO PEOPLE DO WHAT THEY DO

People are often like sheep. They will do, or be led, by what others do. This is especially true if people are following a celebrity or a famous person. This phenomenon is the principle of social proof: determining what is correct in a situation is often determined by what others think is correct. This is often in line with mob mentality. People often get caught up in a situation and go along with the others. Riots often start this way. Someone becomes a leader and does something like throw a stone through a window and many others are soon looking for stones or other objects to throw.

When interviewing people who were caught up in these types of situations the answers are startlingly similar. They just do not know why they acted as they did. They just do not do that sort of thing and they are embarrassed and confused. Some had a vague idea of what it was all about but things progressed, the adrenaline started to flow and they became increasingly active in believing with the crowd. When things settled down and they relooked at their behavior, they could not believe they did what they did. Some did not even know why they did what they did.

Hitler made the comment that it was easier to lead the masses than an individual. This is true because of the social proof principle or the mob mentality principle.

Can the con man utilize this principle? Do leaders in business, athletics, and many other groups use it? Most certainly.

A con man makes a bet in a bar with the guy beside him. It is an individual so the con man is uncertain if the guy will accept or reject. The con guy now, in various ways, involves the guy beside him and another guy near him to get more people involved. It is starting to work. The con guy discusses the situation and soon others are involved supporting each other with statements like can't be done. Such statements reinforce each other in the belief it cannot be done. Instead of one bet, the con guy now has many bets and the sheep are led over the cliff.

Street peddlers do a similar con. They are trying to sell an item. He has his shill come up talk about how wonderful it is. People gather and the shill buys one or maybe several for family members. Others now want it, because someone else wanted it.

Business marketing makes more sales when they advertise how all these people are buying an item. The demand is big. The demand targets others in feeling they also need the item. This happens, as the people making the purchase do not realize it is because others have it. They just think it is a wise purchase.

Let's look at a girl going to a group of men. She catches their attention, stops and talks and maybe even flirts a little. Now the men in the group are in competition with each other and not with the girl. Each will try to outdo the other for the woman's attention. She keeps flirting and soon the men reveal their true personalities. It is up to her to select if she wants to. It is her choice.

It is the same way with the man going into the bar. Put the group of women in competition with each other and then take your pick.

The examples of social proof are endless.

Now what is the key to social proof? The key is the word uncertainty. When people are uncertain they migrate to what others will do and we all know, people love to advise others. If that advice is wrong then it can snowball to destructive consequences to all.

Students in school and college show this tendency when taking tests. If they are uncertain of an answer, they will try to peek for the answer on another's test paper. This is a strange phenomenon because the student has no idea if the other student's answer is right or wrong. The test paper they try to sneak the answer from may be a person who is a complete idiot.

The good con man knows these happenings. He does know the phenomenon and how to use it.

THE INTERNET

Cons and scams were big in the 1800s and early 1900s. Con artists became legends like Titanic Thompson, John Montague, Charles Ponzi, and many others. In the late 1900s things settled down a little but they are still there. In today's market, the internet became a valuable tool to the con artist. The internet can reach so many people, so many suckers.

Two friends set up an internet site that would publish nude pictures of people without having authority from the people involved. With the picture would be the real name, phone number, etc. Many people send naked email photos of themselves through email, Twitter, Facebook, etc. In turn, these two scammers would republish these "private photos" for public usage. With these now public photos, they would offer the name of a lawyer who would have the photos removed from public viewing for 250 dollars. There were no lawyers.

Another scam is the request to give you money.

"Shit, I get almost two of these a day."

Some guy in Africa needs a place to store his money and he/she will split the money if you help him out. Really!

In this one, a girl will enclose a photo of herself. She is poor but has excellent golf potential and wants to come to America to qualify for the pro tour. Naturally, there is a long sob story and will be eternally indebted for your help. The photo may not ever be her but the photo has to be such to show some sex possibility to the man. The photo will not be of an ugly person.

How about the one where the person has inherited a large sum of money but the government is coming to take it away? They quickly need a place to send it for a safekeeping. Send your bank account, address, phone, etc. so it can be readily transferred. Also, send a few dollars for airfare because the money is being forwarded to you, and I am not allowed to make any withdrawals. You are so kind. I love you and may God be good to such a wonderful person.

Love, may mean sex, and God. Bringing God into the scam makes it so legal and so honest. One can trust a believer in God??? And let's not forget the love angle and sex.

E-bay is a big opportunity to swindle as anyone can buy and sell anything. You got something at home and want to get rid of it – sell it on e-bay. A good thing but it is often abused.

"My friend Sam bought a golf car on the internet. Fully equipped with lights, taillights, horns, and all the trimmings for in-city use. He paid 900 dollars. He is still waiting.

A golfer bought some clubs on e-bay and never got them. After a month of waiting, he went through the e-bay and found all the other items the guy had for sale. On all the items, he put a bid in for 20,000,000 dollars. This cancelled all his items as people saw the strange bids and would not deal with the guy. In one week, he got his clubs.

A man paid 275 dollars online for some steaks for a party. Everything was fine, except in a month he receive another shipment of the same stuff. He phones the company and they say that we automatically ship until you tell us not too. However, I said it did not say anything about automatic shipments. I am then told to keep the shipment and they will reduce the bill 40%. I want 100%. Sorry but that is our policy.

A man made an online purchase on golf clubs. It then asks if he would like to buy a wedge for one cent. What the hell? I buy it. Then another item comes on the screen for one cent. He think they must be trying to get rid of this stuff so he buys it because it is only one cent. A month later, I get a bill for the three items and the three items total 490 dollars. The store said the one cent was not the sale price, I was to just try it out, but since I kept it, it is considered bought.

Brehtt goes to his computer to see how many scams are in his e-mail for today only. He reads them.

Good day,

I am ------ from the UK, see attachment of my business proposal. Get back to me with your interest after going through it.

"This guy does not waste time or letters. Trust it????"

Hi Brehtt Bennett!

"An exclamation mark after the greeting???"

Your friend, Re: take the 4-day Challenge ($5,000 A day?) Yes or No (Choose) and, thought that you would be interested in CAROLINE KENNEDY'S WHITE RABBIT ZSA ZSA from Presidential Pet Museum Store.

"Needs help in typing and grammar. Using famous names like the Kennedy family and the movie actress, Zsa Zsa to help bring credibility???? What is a Presidential Pet Museum Store? Is that to make you think in terms of the United States President???"

Our computer has randomly selected 100 people to qualify for exclusive access today. The spots are limited so please click the link below to see if you qualify to access the product today, before everyone else. Your special invitation is below.

"Wow, I am one out of 100. This makes me special. The spots are limited. Do I qualify? If I qualify this makes me special. It must, because the spots are limited. The old scam of making the person feel special and lucky to be involved. I can't believe only one hundred spots. No scam artist is going to limit the number of his scams. He may want you to think that but he will worm every cent he can get."

Positions to work with this GURU are strictly first come; first serve, so you have a huge advantage of the many thousands who will be looking to join tomorrow. Do not miss out on this opportunity to work with this genius. He proves to you how he made $64,062.75 in just 1 DAY.

"And now comes the hurry up part, don't think, don't analyze, just do it. The old scam of everybody is doing it, the social proof theory; if

uncertain do what everyone else is doing. You can't turn down a year's salary in one day of work????

That's it; I cannot read the rest of these scams. Now that I think of it, the email does not say anything on the type of work. Here's another one.

ATTENTION: ATTENTION BENEFICIARY,

I want to inform you that Mr. Frank ----- From African Union Finance Commission {A.U.F.C.} has already sent you $5000.00 US Dollars through Western Union as we have been given the mandate to transfer your full compensation payment total sum of $850.000.00 USD, via Western Union by ministry of finance.

> *"A lot of fancy names for a hint of authenticity but better typing and grammar would help more so."*

I tried reaching you by phone to give you all the information on phone but I could not get through yesterday,

> *"The hell you tried to reach me."*

I decided to email you the MTCN and sender name so that you can pick up the $5000.00 to enable us to send another $5000.00 today. As you know, we will be sending you $5000.00 only per day. It was agreed that you will pay the transfer clearance certificate which sum of $128.00 before the release of the payment to you. Take note of this: you must pay the $128.00 before picking up your first payment.

> *"I never agreed to pay the transfer fee. You're going to pay me $5,000 a day and I have to pay a transfer fee. Take the 128 dollars out of the 5,000 dollars and send me the rest."*

> *"I can't read any more of this."*

My name is Staff Sgt. _____. I am an American soldier that served in the US military in Iraq with the army's 31st infantry division and I have some amount that I want to move out of Iraq which might require some assistance. Please e-mail me at ------- for more details as this email was sent to you from a colleague of mine's email box.

> *"A play on the military, we must help our soldiers. Is this a sympathy play? He does not use his own email so it can't be traced???"*

Hello,

I am _____. I have a charity project I would want you to help me complete due to my health issue. Please respond via ---------- for more details.

> *"Looks like your personal charity. More sympathy with the health issue.*
>
> *I can't take any more of this. I really think the con artist and the scammers, using the internet, are more numerous than ever before."*

CHAPTER 20

THE LADY SPY

It happens again. Natasha gets up from the breakfast table and as she stands, the walls spin around her. She grabs her head and closes her eyes. She falls against the table. With one hand, she pushes away and tries to regroup. It is no use. She can't make it to the bedroom and she collapses on the floor.

She wakes up the next day with the cheeks of her face flush with the floor. She slowly gets up. Goes to the bedroom and lies down in her bed. Now she is worried. She is scared. She does not know what is happening. She has passed out again. She begins to think about brain damage, a possible tumor, or is it some neurological problem.

She thinks maybe she should go to a doctor, but if Russia finds out she has been going to a doctor for neurological problems Russia will do two things, they will drop her as a spy or better still they will kill her. She knows the Russians will fear that in treatment she could reveal her identity and her work to her doctor, who then could pass it on to the United States government. She is damned if she does, and damned if she doesn't. Stress is mounting. Her passing out, her assassination assignment, and Brehtt's lack of love for her. The trauma is overwhelming.

THE CON MAN

ONE OF THOSE DAYS

After going through the internet scams:

> "Amateurs, fucking amateurs. Those internet scams are so revealing. How do people believe them and follow the directions? I'm going out to clear my head."

Brehtt leaves the house and drives to a restaurant and bar for a meal and a few drinks. He sits at the bar and orders a hamburger and fries. While waiting for the order he sips his beer. Soon a beautiful woman, well dressed, ambles into the bar and takes a seat next to Brehtt.

> "Is this my lucky day or is she after a bunch of free drinks with a burger and fries?"

She sits down and nothing is said. She orders a drink. After a period of silence, she asks Brehtt if the burger is worth the price.

"Yes, it is. I come here often just for this meal. If you are short, may I buy you the meal?"

"No thanks, I am not on the make. I'm just in for a quick drink, a meal and I will leave."

"From the looks of the guys around here, they will be sorry to see you go."

"I know, that's why I sat here because you were not ogling me when I came in. It was the safe seat."

"Thanks for the compliment. Does the safe seat mean a safe guy?"

"I think so."

"And what reasoning makes you think that?"

"In my business I have to know men. Men are so predictable and when near or with a pretty woman they become putty, pliable, weak and stupid."

"You must be a psychologist, psychiatrist or possibly a sociologist."

"In a way I am, but I am not trained in these studies. I am a high class prostitute, call girl, escort, - a fuck for money."

Brehtt makes the mistake of sipping his beer when the word prostitute hits his ears. He coughs, chokes, and most of his beer flows out across the bar.

She laughs, "Nice reaction."

"Excuse me. I was caught off guard."

"You know, I think I will have a burger and fries. It looks like a long night but it is my day or maybe night off is better terminology. I will not let you buy me a meal but I will bet you for the meal on something you cannot do."

> "Here comes the scam. Men think they can do everything. It's only for a meal so this may be educational."

"Okay, put your two hands together like you are going to pray, but I warn you praying will not help. All fingers are pointing straight up. Now curl both middle fingers onto the back of the opposite hand. That looks good. Now I will place a quarter between the tips of the two ring fingers. Keeping the palms tight to each other see if you can drop the coin."

> "I know this one. She is trying to con me but I will watch the complete process as to how she presents her con. Con artists like to watch other cons perform to study their presentations, body language, and gift of gab. They also like to study when a con goes silent and when a con talks. The silence gives the mark time to think and the talk gives the mark a time to not think but rush into the scam. Ah, timing is crucial."

"I can't."

"I know, it can't be done. So cutie, order my meal."

"With pleasure."

They continue talking and joking and she finally reveals a bet she made with a drunk rich man. She bet the rich guy $2,000, her nightly charge, that she could piss higher up on a wall than the rich guy could. He just had to use the same stance as she did. If she won, she would get the 2,000 dollars. If he won he would get the free night with her. They go out of the bar and into the adjacent alley with many following in tow.

She places her hands on her hips and pisses on the wall. He laughs along with the other spectators. He drops his pants and shorts, grabs his penis. She grabs his arm and says just like me, hands on hips, no hands. He pisses on the ground and his shoes.

They eat their meal and it is getting late. They are on their last drink when she reaches over and grabs his hand.

"I am also a fortuneteller and I can read you mind."

> "Here comes the big scam. She is going to try and take me for 2,000 dollars."

She takes his hand and strokes the palm.

"Ahha, you like that. I can feel your vibrations. I bet your penis is lifting. You're thinking you would like to spend the night with me but not for 2,000 dollars. Now you're thinking it's only 2,000. It's only money. Maybe I can negotiate. Your penis is rising higher and the higher it rises the less you are concerned about the money."

Now she raises his hand to her mouth, places the middle finger in her mouth, gives it a little sucking action, takes it out and puts the finger in Brehtt's mouth for an exchange of saliva, the love juice. All this time her eyes never leave Brehtt's eyes.

Brehtt is off in dreamland. "And what does a beautiful woman like you do on the day off?"

"Fuck, and fuck some more. It is my day off so I cannot charge you. How about a free one?"

HOME REPAIR SCAMS

> *"Logically these could be a good deal since the reasoning is sound, but often the quality of the work is terrible."*

The deal is that they are in the area with left over material so they can do a quick and good job immediately. Here is how it goes.

A truck drives along the street with many houses and looks for a driveway that is aging and need some repair. They spot one and one of the men goes to the door of the homeowner and says that they were down the street repairing a driveway and as we were leaving, we noticed your driveway could use a little repair. The homeowner, wife, or resident at the time knows the guy is telling the truth because the driveway does need repair.

The guy then explains how he can offer a special price, well below normal because they are in the area with the material. A little extra work will be good. Because of the price, it has to be a cash deal because he has to pay the extra help immediately. The help cannot read or write but they understand cash. The cash is given before the work starts.

> *"Of course, this is not true because the crew is usually family members, relatives or close friends."*

Agreement is made and they do the work. They haul out the material and coat the driveway. They do not even sweep the cracks clean. It is a rush job and sometimes they drive off without even doing anything. Sometimes they drive off saying they need to get some material. They never come back.

This procedure is done on other repairs. Deals are arranged when the workers say they are in need of money so they will do the work for the cost of materials.

"Here we go again with the sympathy con."

Here are some cons.

Driveways were blacktopped with crankcase oil, which is washed away with the rain or sprinklers. Paint jobs for outside the house ended up on the lawn when washed down by the rain. Tree planting was done by cutting branches off trees and sticking them in the ground. They never grew. They soon wilted and died. People in these scam had to move around to different cities for their own safety.

Here's one where the con gets into the house as a furnace inspector for the city's safety program. He is dressed in clothes that are logoed with the company name. On inspecting the furnace, he is able to make claims, fraudulent claims, to the unaware owner or wife. The furnace is old, in bad shape, could blow up any time. In fact, he is surprised it is still working.

"Here comes the hook."

It just so happens, he tells the owner that he has an excellent furnace that will fit in here just perfect and he will sell it for cost. He just wants to get rid of it. He collects the money and leaves. The owner never does see the furnace.

An encyclopedia salesman had an excellent scam for sales. And why not, push the education factor and people have a hard time refusing. One principal did refuse.

The salesman would go to the local school principal's home and talk to the principal about the educational value of the books. The principal would agree and in a short while they were both together on the same page on the value of such books. The salesman would ask if he liked them so much would he like to buy a set. The principal would refuse saying he has a set in the school library. The salesman then pushes the idea that having the book at home is so convenient.

Now comes the deal. The salesman says that since you like the books so much I will give you this demo set free.

"Does he take it or does he walk away?"

The principal does not take the deal. The salesman pushes for a reason and so the principal says that if I take the deal, you will go around telling everyone that they should buy the books for their kids. You are using me to promote your sales and commission. I cannot be a part of that.

"A principal with principle."

Florida is ripe with cons. They are all over. One reason for settling in Florida is that the Cayman Islands are nearby, one hour by air. They have banks, like the Swiss banks that will not release information on their accounts. If a scammer is in trouble, he can declare bankruptcy to his clients, hop over to the Caymans, and live out his life in luxury. Not a bad deal.

After lunch, Brehtt looks for his Kindle.

"Damn it, it was right here. I need some new tricks for that party tonight. Ahh, it is on the bed. I was reading last night from my Kindle and laid it down beside me on the bed. When I got up, I threw the covers and I guess it covered the Kindle. I got it now."

He picks it up and lies down on the bed. With a few screen taps, he gets his book on mental magic tricks. He reads the various tricks and then replays them in his mind. The replays are to get a good picture, just in real life, so that he can make sure of his every move and possible counter moves by his viewers.

He's got all he needs and then falls asleep on the bed.

He wakes up much later. Gets dressed and off to the party. There is a large gathering at the party of his friends, acquaintances and a few strangers. Entering his mind is that this is not the type of place for taking bets. This is just a fun evening in which he is reminded of his prostitute friend of a few days ago when asked what she does on her day off, she replies, "Fuck, but not for money." Therefore, Brehtt is at the party to entertain only with no objective to hustle the partygoers. We do the same things during the workweek but not for money on the days off. With this reasoning, Brehtt is just in a casual, easy and unconcerned attitude.

The party house is crowded with a friendly attitude in the air. He walks around greeting people. Naturally, he looks around for the women.

> *"This party is a little dangerous to be hitting on married women. I am scared of husbands. Why mess with married women and the possible dangers when there are so many single and divorced women out there who are very accommodating? Women who are separated can also be dangerous as for some reason their husbands still think they own the woman even though the separation is legal. Divorced and separated husbands do not want their exes going out on dates and having sex with others. They just can't let go. They have jealousy fits in thinking that their ex is having fun and sex. Perhaps more fun than they are."*

After an hour or so, an old friend walks up and asks if he's got any new tricks.

"Naww, nothing new."

A woman standing next to him says, "You're a trickster. You do tricks. Are you a male prostitute? How much do you charge? If I get my husband's permission can we do a few tricks?"

This gets Brehtt laughing and soon everyone around is wondering why he's laughing. They move in closer as Brehtt replies, "Not that kind of tricks. I'm a half-assed magician and . . . Almost like a chant; several people do the "Show us a trick..." chant.

> *"I am going to let them think I am mulling over their request, build the anticipation. The greater the anticipation the greater they fall for the trick."*

"Okay, let's try this one. I haven't done this in years so let's give it a try."

"We need three confederates. One is to take a dollar bill, crumple it into a ball and hold it in his fist. The next one is to do the same except with a five dollar bill and the last one is also too repeat but use a ten dollar bill."

"Now put this blindfold on me," as he pulls out his handkerchief. The lady beside him puts the blindfold on to obscure his vision.

"I cannot see you people but I can guess the amount of the bill in the clenched fist of the hand that covers the bill completely."

To the lady beside him he says, "Have one of them step forward and I will identify the bill in his or her hand."

"You have the ten dollar bill."

The hand opens and a crumpled ten-dollar bill is shown.

They gasp in silence.

"Next."

"I now have a 50% chance on this one but it is easy as 100%. You have the one dollar bill."

The crumpled bill is a one dollar bill.

Another gasp.

"And now the clincher, the one left is the five dollar bill. Am I close?"

No more gasps, they laugh.

"Show us another one."

"Maybe later as my mind needs a rest."

> "Once again, the simplicity is overwhelming. The trick is not needing to see the hand or the confederate. Blindfolds leave an open area

under the eye so that with a blindfold in place one can look straight down, not ahead or sideways but straight down. With this observation, I ask one of them to step forward. By looking straight down I recognize his or her shoes and that is all I need. When the people put the bill in their hand, I made note of their shoes. Their shoes identify the one, five and ten dollar holders. This is so simple it is almost embarrassing. Simplicity is often what throw people off in the analysis of the trick. They look way past the simplicity of the trick."

The party is going on and everyone is drunk or nearly drunk. The mood is joyous and safe with no one getting obnoxious or violent. A group approach Brehtt again for another trick. Brehtt agrees.

Brehtt asks his host for a small compass. As he waits for the compass, he excuses himself from his friends saying he has to go to the toilet but will be right back as the compass should be ready by then.

He returns and sits at the table, places the compass in front of him, lifts one leg onto the other knee.

"Now, my hands are empty, no long sleeves to hide anything. Now, can anyone make the needle on the compass move? You cannot use any metal object or similar item. Sally, the lady who called him a male prostitute and has been following him around tries it. She concentrates, moves her hand, wiggles her butt, but nothing works. Others try to no avail.

Brehtt raises his hands high. "My thought powers will move the compass. My brain will send out alpha brain waves to the needle. The needle will jump, spin, and do strange things. Now give me a few seconds to charge the brain and locate the alpha brain wave site. . . now . . ."

The needle moves, jumps and spins. Again, the group is aghast.

"It is amazing what a little magnet will do. I went to the bathroom and put the magnate in the toe of my shoe. When I crossed or lifted

my leg on top of the other leg the magnet was directly under the table and under the compass. As my foot moves, the needle moves. Brilliant. Again so simple."

It is 2:00 am and things are winding down. Brehtt starts to leave but is stopped by Sally, a little tipsy but still in control.

"Slow down, guy. I'm going home with you."

Brehtt is taken aback and then starts to laugh. "That would be lovely but your husband may shoot me or at least object."

"Oh no, we have an open marriage, no problem." Brehtt smiles but walks away.

CHAPTER 21

THE SPY LADY

Natasha continues her surveillance of Jim Sloan. She wants to pick up where he goes what he does after their daily sessions. Usually he goes home to his wife. Natasha is there at the Senate building when he leaves. Naturally, he doesn't see her. She watches closely. Where does he park his car? What route does he take to go home? Her training has taught her how to follow without being detected. She does this for a week and finds he is consistent with the route he takes. Since her Lamborghini would be easily recognized. She rents a car for surveillance.

After a week of surveillance, she feels she has his routine down pretty good. Now that she has a routine, she starts picking for details. Where is the best spot to kill him? Where is the least traveled areas by automobile and or by pedestrians? What are the time frames for the action to be carried out? She does all this at home with her maps highlighters and colored pencils and pens. While doing this she is hit with an ironic thought. How wonderful it is of Google maps to help her carry out an assassination.

THE CON MAN

HISTORY LESSON

It's a study day. It's raining. No golf. The country club is closed tonight. No cards. It's just the kindle and me.

> *"This is what I want. A book on the history of the con. A few taps and the email book downloads. God this is neat. I love this high-tech shit."*

No one knows when the con started but one would think the cave man and cave woman had the jump. In all probability, the cave man conned another cave man into betting the mark for his dinosaur leg. The mark lost and has lost ever since.

The cave woman was just as good when she created the possibility for sex and the mark lost his food and hunting club while the cave woman vanished.

The cons flourished throughout history but until records and documents became fashionable, little is known about the details of such cons. Prior to writings and the printing press knowledge was passed by word of mouth and folklore. As we know, these stories became exaggerated and distorted through time.

Wherever money or other valuable items became prominent, the scam artists came out of the woodwork. Some of these artists made more money than the actual workers. In the California and Alaska golf rushes, the scam artists did extremely well, better than some of the miners. During the age of discovery, with explorers finding new products and foods the scammers were ready with bogus and fraudulent products claiming they got them in their worldly travel. Tea, spices, pottery, etc. became profitable. When the nuclear age came, false uranium was also utilized.

This is why in the 1920s the famous W. C. Crosby said that confidence is a business and like all businesses, it changes and conforms to the conditions of the times. This is true as we have seen with the internet.

When something new to come along the demand is great the scammers will offer the product for a much lower price, which gives the scammer a 100% profit because the victims never get the product.

Recorded frauds started to be documented in the early 1700s and up until the early 1900s, it was considered the 'age of the con' because it was so prevalent. The cons ruled the world. They were all over the globe.

John Law showed the later cons how to sell bogus stocks back in the early 1700s. He worked with Louise XIV to balance the French economy but duped them instead. His stock was the Mississippi Company in the USA. He duped investors here also.

Robert Harley almost ruined England with bogus stocks for the South Seas Company. These guys were the forerunners of future similar scams. Charles Ponzi name became the title for all future style of frauds called a Ponzi.

Women also followed with Therese Dauignac, in late 1700s, who claimed she had 20 million of inheritance from the American industrialist Robert Henry Crawford. As she flirted with high society, she was able to borrow large sums on the claim of her 20 million left to her by Crawford for caring for him and nursing him back to health. Oddly enough, she was believed because of her spending and luxurious life style. In time, investigation proved she had no inheritance so she suffered a short prison sentence.

Daniel Drew, a religious fanatic con man, was on a cattle drive in 1815. He ordered his men to not let the cattle drink water for three days and that salt be mixed in their feed. Just before reaching his station, he let the cows drink all the water they wanted which was quite a lot since they were so dehydrated. The cows, now enormously bloated, were weighed. Water is heavy and so the cattle had good weight. Cattle are paid by the weight. He collected his money than disappeared. The next day the cows were sick and rib-thin.

Drew was an illiterate but he did swindle the rich and famous Commodore Cornelius Vanderbilt. With his money from the cow scam, he made bogus securities and bonds, sawdust and meat packing firms, dilapidated inns and ferry lines. He was getting Vanderbilt to buy him out which he did. Vanderbilt paid an overpriced fee to get him out of the business because he wanted it. Vanderbilt was taken, and taken good.

Drew also devised a plan to get Vanderbilt to buy into Eire Railroad stock. Vanderbilt did and he thought he had the market cornered. However, the more stock he bought the more stock appeared. Drew had a printing press printing up more bogus shares. Vanderbilt kept buying but could never corner the market because more shares kept popping up and Drew kept printing more false shares.

Jay Gould and Big Jim Fisk, former associates of Drew, worked a scam on cornering the gold market with the unknowing help of President Grant. They never succeeded but they did direct several millions of dollars into their pockets.

The real-estate cons were innovated by Colonel Novena, a man adept at impersonations and conning money out of people. His biggest swindle was in New York when he optioned several lots in underdeveloped area of New York. He then promoted how this area would build an elaborate building called the Novena Building. He had great architectural plans for a structure of magnificence. A building of wonder. People tried to buy into his plans with offers of 20 times the value of the optioned land of which Novena had not paid for. He left New York with more money than he would ever need.

The real-estate cons are still going because prime land (in the everglades) in Florida is still for sale. Ocean front sales are still up for sale in Arizona. The list is endless. Was this a scam or a joke, whatever, some person made a pile of money selling pet rocks? And, when the Berlin Wall came down souvenir pieces were sold at good prices although the pieces probably came from an old construction site down the road. Cement and rocks look the same in Germany and in the USA.

Sofia Lyons was the first big American con woman. A former whore, she associated with New York's underworld. She stole one million in confidence games, extremely good money back then. She retired as a columnist for the New York World newspaper as the first society columnist. Now the society columnists or gossip columnists are all over, especially in New York and Los Angeles.

Three-card monte and the shell game may well be the oldest cons in America. They were big at fairs and carnivals and along the Mississippi where the riverboats and gambling floated up and down the river. Nowadays, these cons operate everywhere on street corners, parks, wherever people are.

Three-card monte involved two aces and a queen. The three cards are placed in a row face down. The con then moves the cards around and the mark is to pick the queen. If he picks the queen, he is lucky or he is being set-up for a bigger bet. Sometimes a confederate will reach over when the con turns his back to get a drink and bends the corner of the queen. The mark does not know it is a set up. The con returns from his drink and moves the card around but straightens the corner of the queen and bends the corner of another card. The mark picks the bent corner card and it is not the queen. He has been had.

The shell game involves three half-walnut shells or objects of a similar nature. A pea or small round object of similar size is used. Often the pea is a small round piece of sponge because it slides under a shell very easily because the sponge can be pressed down. This means the shell does not have to lift very high to get the pea under.

Like the three-card monte the shells are switched around and the mark picks the shell the pea is under. Like the monte if he picks the pea, he is lucky or the con is setting him up for a bigger bet. More than likely it is a set up.

Canada Bill won fortunes with his three-card monte but lost it on the faro card game. His friend tried to pull him away from the game but was unable to; even though he told Bill the game was rigged. It was crooked. Canada Bill came up with the classic line, still popular today, "I know, but it's the only game in town." This is kind of reasoning like when they asked the guy who did the Brinks robbery why he robbed the bank, "Because that is where the money is."

Along this time the Spanish Prisoner game was popular and the strange con of printing counterfeited money and then selling it. Great fortunes where raised doing this.

The Banco game flourished in the old west. It was a little more complicated than the three-card monte but they still liked it. A cloth was laid out and if the game was with dice, there were fourteen spaces on the cloth. The game was mostly played with cards. There were forty-two numbered spaces, one blank space. Bets would be placed and like the shell game, and three-card monte, the mark could not win.

Around this time, particularly in the old west, the gold brick swindle was in vogue. Fake gold bricks were sold were sold for big money.

The Magic Wallet was a famous con that Elmer Mead originated. For a time he was considered the most successful con in the business. Mead lived a strict religious life even though he was one of the greatest con artists. His moniker or nickname was, "The Christian Kid," or the "Christ Kid." Nicknames or monikers are common in the confidence community. Most never used their real name and most had nicknames.

After deserting his wife, he hooked up with a woman called "Frisco Kate" or "Klondike Kate". They were a successful duo who hit and run. His Magic Wallet con was a clever con in getting people to invest in private big con deals. The investments varied and were on a magnificent and impressive scale. The investments were for large stadiums, shopping centers, etc.

The wallet was a come on full of money, legal data, etc. it was placed for the mark to find it. It would be found and then the owner (a shill), acting hysterical about losing the wallet would get the wallet back. The mark finding the wallet would be led to believe something big was coming up and he wanted to invest in it. He knew this from seeing the insides of the wallet. An investment was made. The mark was taken. Mead earned several million with this con.

The con was so good that it became common in the trade. It was the forerunner to several other cons like the "pigeon drop" which was one of the most lucrative cons. The pigeon drop is a short con for quick money. A purse is found, loaded with money. Two confederates and a mark seem to find it at the same time. They debate on what to do. They decide to let the mark keep the money for say 30 days and if no one claims it then they will split the money. For safety and trust, the mark is conned into giving the two confederates a sum of money, usually 1,000 dollars, for safekeeping of the money. 1,000 dollars is a good deal when the mark will be looking after ten times that as usually 10,000 or more is in the purse. The deal is made. They all go separate ways. Soon the mark finds that the money in the purse is paper cut to money size.

America went through a period of bogus medical frauds, mail order cons, sometimes called snake oil treatments. Such purchases could cure anything. You name it, we cure it. It was a profitable business. With the internet and online ads and emails, it seems to be coming back. The claim of research verifying the effectiveness of the medicine seems to make the medicine believable. Studies are twisted and manipulated. Drug companies are under fire with false claims even today. The FDC does not test the drugs. They rely on the research by the drug company. Have you noticed how many drugs have had to be recalled because of people dying or suffering from serious side effects? Remember Vioxx?

During this time period, a brilliant non-medical scam appeared. This con appeared in over 200 newspapers in 1882. The ad offered a rare portrait of President Garfield. The assassinated Garfield was loved by many because of his style of death. The ad was for an authorized full color portrait by Government's expert engravers of the late President Garfield. The portrait was USA government approved. Send one dollar for each portrait.

When the portrait was received, there was great disappointment, as the portrait was a five-cent postage stamp. The advertisement seems to be legit as the stamp was government approved.

Here's another one. In the late 1890s, an ad appeared in newspapers and magazines. The gist of the ad was that if moths bothered you they would furnish a solution. Just send 50 cents in postage stamps, legal tender. When the solution arrived the mark was told to dampen the article in question with kerosene, and if need be soak it thoroughly, add one lighted match. This should solve your problem.

THE POOL ROOM

> "Ya know, I think I might like to play some pool this evening. A little change of pace."

Off he goes to his familiar pool room where many hustlers, would be hustlers, think they are hustlers, and no way hustlers congregate.

He walks in says hello to a few friends and sits at the bar waiting for a game.

In twenty minutes, Donny "The Mouth" approaches Brehtt.

"Hey Dude. Want a game""

> "Yes I want a game but not with you. You are a pain in the ass, crybaby when losing, egotistical, and incompetent. You are just looking to beat me to get your money back from the many times I skunked you."

"Well, I wasn't really intending to play. I was just going to have a beer." Brehtt quietly answers.

"You scared of me? You were lucky last time. I think you are just chicken shit. All talk. An arrogant asshole . . ."

By now, there is a large group gathering around watching the challenge.

"Table number 5 is open. Take it if you have the money. Otherwise, fuck off," a defiant Donny threatens.

"Ohhh," the group sensing bitter rivalry as they rush and surround table 5.

Brehtt is in no rush as he continues to sip his drink.

"I'm going to irritate that asshole to the point of his hands shaking and his brain shaking."

The group is waiting and getting restless. Donny is yelling at Brehtt and mumbling under his breath. He is getting irritated.

"Come on, chicken shit."

"I'm not finished with my drink."

"Fuck the drink." Donny walks over to Brehtt grabs the drink and dumps it in the wastebasket. "You finished your drink now."

Brehtt gets up and moves to the number 5 table. When he gets there he says, "Excuse me, but I have to get my cue stick out of the car."

He walks past Donny, smiles at him and continues out the door. By now, Donny is boiling. His face is blushed red and wrinkled from frowning.

Brehtt returns to see that all the tables are now cleared as all are around table 5. Slowly he opens his cue case, screws his cue to together. Does a few stretches of no value except to irritate Donny. The first game bet is for 100 dollars.

The game starts and Brehtt lets Donny break. The balls scatter but nothing goes in a pocket. It is Brehtt's turn so he tells Donny that, "Because he is so mad he won't be able to sink a shot for the entire game."

"You're on, how much?"

"I say a hundred because I think you have no confidence in your ability. You are scared to go to high."

This brings a few gasps and whispers from the gallery.

"You cheap sniveling punk," as he reaches into his pocket and pulls out 500 dollars and throws it on the table. Brehtt covers him.

Brehtt walks around for his shot, takes his time, adding drama, sets up to the cue ball, strikes it and knocks the 8-ball in the pocket. The game is officially over when the 8-ball is sunk. Donny has not even taken a shot. Brehtt loses the game of 100 dollars but wins the bet of 500 dollars for a 400-dollar profit.

The gallery is giggling and laughing. Donny is furious.

"Donny, double or nothing for a chance to get your money back," says Brehtt.

Brehtt lays a pool cue across the table and tells Donny if he can roll a ball under the pool cue.

"You're fucking nuts; it can't be done."

"I can do it. Try the cue ball; it is slightly smaller than the rest of the balls."

He tries and verifies it can't be done."

"Give me my money."

"Can't do that, Donny. The money is mine."

Brehtt takes the cue ball, walks around the table, again doing the drama bit, reaches down and rolls the ball under the table, which in turn is under the cue stick.

Brehtt collects another 1,000 dollars. The gallery is beside themselves with high fives, yells, laughs and slapping of each other. They love it because they love seeing the big mouth get his due.

"Donny, I will play you for 1,000 dollars. You get unlimited shots and you still won't be able to sink every ball without scratching."

"I never scratch."

"We'll see, every ball now."

Donny goes and plays his shots. He sinks all the balls except the cue ball.

"Okay, I win."

"Sorry Donny, the bet was every ball and the cue ball is still left on the table. Sink the cue ball and you scratch."

Brehtt's pocket is now overflowing in cash.

"Donny, I will give you 50 dollars if I can't sink the next two shots."

"Yeah, yeah, let's see it."

Brehtt takes out 50 dollars and lays it on the table. At the long end of the table, closest to the spot on the table where the balls are racked. He puts a ball in front of each pocket and has Donny stand at the end of the table and stretch his arms and place a finger on top of each ball.

Donny, hold the fingers on the ball so that the cue ball cannot knock the balls in the hole in one shot. Donny then places a quarter on the ball rack mark, goes to the other long end of the table and sets up the cue ball. He strokes the cue ball to the quarter the ball jumps up and strikes Donny in the groin. Donny buckles up and goes down. The gallery is in hysterics. It seems to be part of human nature that when a man gets hit in the groin it is funny. It is almost automatic as all men feel the pain.

Brehtt leaves the money for Donnie and starts to walk out the door. Donny stops him, looks around and says:

"I do not know what to say or do, and I am ashamed of myself. You taught me a good lesson." Brehtt puts his arm around his shoulder as he approaches the door. Reaches into his pocket, pulls out some of the money, about 1,000 dollars, and gives it back to Donny. Donny smiles, Brehtt laughs and both depart with more respect for each other than they ever had.

MORE HISTORY

After his poolroom escapades, he goes home, jumps in bed and reads more of his history of cons.

These two cons, Victor Lustig and George Parker, must be among the best in the world.

Victor Lustig was renowned as the Man who Sold the Eiffel Tower. People had heard that it was done but hardly anyone knows who the guy was. This man was extremely brazen, confident and worked a glib tongue. He started out selling a device that could print money at the rate of one bill every 6 hours. People paid enormous amounts for the machine that only had two one-hundred dollar bills hidden in the machine. Once these bills slid out blank paper came out. Since the machine only slid a bill out every six hours, Lustig was long gone.

In 1925, France was recovering from the war and the Eiffel Tower's maintenance was very expensive. The tower was never meant to be permanent but just for the World's Fair in Paris. The newspaper was discussing the expenses and possible removable of the tower. This gave Listig an idea. He forged government credentials and invited six scrap metal dealers to a secret meeting in a hotel. Since Paris could not afford to keep the tower, they would sell it for scrap. He stressed secrecy for all dealings, as the public may not like the idea of the tower's removal.

Lustig took the dealers in a limousine to tour the tower. One of the dealers, Andre Poisson was convinced that the tale was legitimate and he handed over the money. Later he realized he had been conned, he was too embarrassed to tell the police. One month later, Lustig returned to Paris to try the scam again. This time it was reported to the police. Luckily, Lustig managed to escape.

George Parker also pulled swindles that are easily remembered but his name is not.

Parker was one of the most audacious con men in American history. He made his living selling New York's public landmarks to unwary tourists. His favorite object for sale was the Brooklyn Bridge, which he sold twice a week for years. He convinced his marks that they could make a fortune by controlling access to the roadway. Many times police had to remove naive buyers from the bridge as they tried to erect toll barriers.

Other public landmarks he sold included the original Madison Square Garden, the Metropolitan Museum of Art, Grant's Tomb, and the Statue of Liberty. George had many different methods for making his sales. When he sold Grant's Tomb, he would often pose as the general's grandson. He even set up a fake "office" to handle his real estate swindles. He produced impressive forged documents to prove that he was the legal owner of whatever property he was selling.

Parker was convicted of fraud three times. After his third conviction on December 17, 1928, he was sentenced to a life term at Sing Sing Prison. He spent the last eight years of his life behind bars. He was popular among guards and fellow inmates who enjoyed hearing of his exploits. George is remembered as one of the most successful con men in the history of the United States, as well as one of history's most talented hoaxers. His exploits have passed into popular culture, giving rise to phrases such as "and if you believe that, I have a bridge to sell you", a popular way of expressing a belief that someone is gullible.

"It is amazing how he could sell so many famous landmarks."

Eduardo de Valfierno was an Argentine con man who masterminded the theft of the Mona Lisa. Valfierno paid several men to steal the work of art from the Louvre, including museum employee Vincenzo Peruggia. On August 21, 1911, Peruggia hid the Mona Lisa under his coat and simply walked out the door.

"So much for security!"

Before the heist took place, Valfierno commissioned French art restorer and forger Yves Chaudron to make six copies of the Mona Lisa. The forgeries were then shipped to various parts of the world, readying them for the buyers he had lined up. Here is the brilliancy of the plan. The forgeries were shipped before the Mona Lisa was stolen. Valfierno knew once the Mona Lisa was stolen it would be more difficult to smuggle copies past customs. After the heist, the copies were delivered to their buyers, each thinking they had the original, which had just been stolen for them. Because Valfierno just wanted to sell forgeries, he only needed the original Mona Lisa to disappear and never contacted Peruggia again after the crime. Eventually Peruggia was caught trying to sell the painting and it was returned to the Louvre in 1913.

Romance scams were big in the 1800s and 1900s but perhaps not as big as the romance dating on the internet. The ploys are numerous but they all boil down to lonely people looking for love, friendship and even marriage. The mark is led to believe that the future is bright and often will help the con with money for a car, entertainment, country club dues, etc. By the time the mark realizes something is not right, the con is gone. Women are often the marks in the romance scams.

Women are not alone in the romance scams. The badger game extortion is often perpetrated on married men. The mark is deliberately coerced into a compromising position, a supposed affair or a sex position, and then threatened with public exposure of his acts unless blackmail money is paid.

The Thai gem scam involves a team of con men and helpers who tell a tourist in Bangkok of an opportunity to earn money by buying duty-free jewelry and having it shipped back to the tourist's home country. . This scam has been operating for 20 years in Bangkok, and is said to be protected by Thai police and politicians. A similar scam usually runs in parallel for custom-made suits. Many tourists are hit by conmen touting both goods.

> "This is not unusual. Con artists like dealing with tourists from out of city, out of state and out of country. Tourists like to buy souvenirs and are usually freer in spending money when touring or vacationing. Tourists are conned and then gone."

Insurance fraud includes a wide variety of schemes. The most common scams are the sore back and neck damage. Some people carry a neck brace in the event of an accident. Lawyers even tell their clients to wear the brace. Neck pain and back pain are hard to prove even with x-rays as the pain may be there but will not show up on the film. Claiming neck and back pain is to the victim's advantage.

A common scam is for a con artist to drive alone with someone behind him. A schill will then cut in front of the con artist forcing the con to slam on the brakes, which in turn causes the car behind the con to ram into the back of the con's car. The shill naturally is long gone and the car that hit the con's car is responsible for the accident, not only in damages but also in medical damages.

Arson is another big insurance scam. Need the money, burn the house down.

This insurance scam was in 1811 and is the first recorded scam of this nature. Edward Tinker, the captain of a commercial vessel, scuttles his ship off Roanoke Island and fakes his insurance claim for the ship and cargo. A crewmember ratted on him, so he killed him, got caught and was hanged.

Some people have been known to park their car in large parking lots with lots of parked cars at all- night operations, like factories. They report the car stolen. It is not found because no one checks parking lots much. In a short time, the con gets his insurance money.

Let's not forget the little old lady shopping in a grocery store who spills some liquid on the floor, then lies down, yells and moans. In time, she hobbles up and is taken to the emergency ward and checked. Luckily no severe damage. She then sues the store for negligence and settles out of court. One lady in the Buffalo, NY area made a good living settling out of court.

Antivirus software also has the swindle of offering free scans of the computers. Naturally, they find your computer is in big danger and needs cleaning, but for a price. The user does not know if the computer needs cleaning so the price is paid. The cleanup was quick and easy because there was nothing wrong to begin with.

How about the modern scam of phishing. An email comes in from what looks like a legal company or a company that the receiver has actually done business with. It often starts with updating your profile. What they are actually doing is phishing for personal information to later scam you. Some even ask for a credit card number and get it.

Fake casting agent fraud is an old theatre, movies, operas, etc. con. The confidence artist poses as a casting agent for a modeling agency searching for new talent. The aspiring model is told that they will need a portfolio or comp card. The mark will pay an upfront fee to have photos and create their portfolio, after which they will be sent on their way in the hope that their agent will find them work in the following weeks. Of course, they never hear back from the confidence artist.

> *"People trying to break into the performing arts are gullible in hoping this is their break. The casting couch, was and still is, often used on adults, teens and children. These procedures are still big in the porn industry."*

Here's a neat scam. A guy offers to buy a large, older hotel. He spends days going through the books, asking pertinent questions of the owners and finally, after a week of deliberations, he offers a million dollars for the establishment. The owners agree and the guy gives them a check for one-third of the price and a promissory note to pay the balance in thirty days.

The guy appears to be a reputable buyer as all cons seem to be, so the owner hands over the keys, and he is now in possession of the hotel. A few days later, the check he wrote as down payment, bounces. He makes an excuse. It bounces again. He comes up with more and more stories. The former owners keep re-depositing the check. Then they call in their attorneys and accountants. The guy has the keys to the hotel. He is technically in physical and legal possession of the premises. It gets closer and closer to the date when the remainder of the money is due, and he cannot even cover the original check he wrote. The sellers continue to think that the transaction will occur as he continues to tell them to "re-deposit it." Having re-deposited the check to the point where any ordinary fool would have given up, they sit over in their attorneys' office with their accountants, pondering: "Should we try it again?"

Finally, somebody figures out that for one month the guy has been walking through the entire hotel, the bars and casinos, every two or three hours and cleaning out the cash registers. How much simpler can it be? It was theft with a passable civil patina that protected the man for a month. Instead of walking in there every two or three hours and pulling a gun and holding up every bar and restaurant cashier, walking out and waiting a few more hours before coming back to pull a gun and hold them up again, he just took over the hotel.

The con was so crude, so simple, that they could not see it.

How about these laughable cons. During a bad beet season, many farmers were hit hard. The government examined the problem but came up with nothing. An entrepreneur saw a possibility. He put advertisements in papers and magazines saying that for one dollar he will send printed instructions to solve the beet problems.

Thousands answered the ad. "Plant your feet firmly, take hold of the tops, and pull," was the answer.

> "Well, that raised the beets. Isn't it amazing how so many cons are simple in the wording? We saw this in the poolroom scams.

One man offered a device to make short people taller. People sent in their money for instructions. The instructions were a picture of a torture rack in which the body was stretched. Not much work for the 50,000 dollars he took in.

Love ads go back a long way. One ad encourages those who are fond of the society of young men, even though they may lack some beauty or lack training in this area can learn it easily. If you want to make an impression, send in one dollar for instructions. The instructions were simple – sit in a pan of dough.

> "Here we go again in how a word can be so misunderstood. The instructions were right in that it did create an impression."

This one may well be the forerunner to the many books out now on attracting women, how to do it, how to make them love you, how to get them in bed with you, etc. these same procedures are on the internet by self-appointed love gurus and love doctors.

This forerunner ad tells how you can get the secret to love and how to get a woman to love you. The procedure is based on scientific principles. Send in one dollar for instructions.

The response is not scientific. It just says to be clean and neat, do not drink alcohol, be generous, be brave, dignified, use flattery, and do not be bashful. This response is signed with Yours for Suckers.

> "A little hostility in calling the guy who sent him the money a sucker?"

Lots of money was made on this one back in the early 1900s. Newspaper ads flooded the market on how to double your money. One dollar becomes two dollars. Five dollars become 10 dollars and so on. Wealthy men are doing it.

> "The old social proof theories of others doing it, so it must be ok."

For 2 dollars, you can receive the secret. The secret is to convert your money into bills, and fold them.

After the civil war, the confederate money was worthless except for some who advertised that for two dollars they could convert your two dollars into 50 and send you the 50. The fifty returned was a 50-dollar confederate bill.

Here's another ad con. People were looking for jobs so the ads said they were looking for good workers and many had success in getting jobs. Send in two dollars for a list. The list received was a page from the local newspaper want ads. Nowadays they use the internet.

How about the guy who in 1935 offered information on becoming an airline pilot career. Jobs and money were scarce so many applied by sending in their two dollars. They received a brochure on Army Air Corps training program.

This one has no love for the con. A street peddler in New York City was selling diet pills. The pills did work and he had satisfied customers for a short time, until months later when the people found out they were ingesting tapeworm eggs.

A boy in Nigeria placed ads in many USA newspapers looking for pen pals. He got them. In time, he asked for four dollars and an old pair of pants and in return, he would send ivory, and gems, which he said, were common in Nigeria. Four dollars and pants were sent but no gems were returned. Postal inspectors traced the con but could do nothing. The con was a 14-year-old boy and underage for prosecuting. Cons are all ages.

CHAPTER 22

THE SPY LADY

Natasha takes a rental car and goes over the areas on her maps. She is looking for escape routes that would not be on the maps, like alleyways that are not blocked off, like entrances that are not locked and are always open, like windows for apartments or businesses. Apartment windows usually have people in the evenings and at night and are able to see out onto the streets. Businesses are usually over at business hours and see little of evening action on the streets. All these things, details, are so important. Finally, she goes home.

After a restless night, she wakes up, groggy, bitter, and hateful because of what she has to do. She has no choice. She has to kill Jim Sloan or the Russians would kill her. Not much of a choice. It is nice to stay alive. She struggles out of bed. Gets dressed in slacks, sneakers and sweatshirt. She packs her knapsack with her assassination tools of poison darts and a poison walking cane tip. The poison darts are loaded into the BG 9 mm blowgun. The BG 9 works like a blowgun but the dart is ejected by a gas cartridge. The gun is a long tube that is strapped to the forearm from the elbow to the hand. This style is easier to conceal in that long sleeve shirt or sport jacket can hide the implement in the sleeve of the shirt or jacket. The hand will cover the darts release. This method is better than the blowgun where the assassin blows air through the tube. The blowgun is much too visible to the public. The BG 9 gun is very hard to detect or be seen by a witness. A button releases the dart. The walking cane also has a trigger in the handle to release poison through a needle at the end of the cane.

Natasha does not want to get too close to Senator Sloan to use the cane. The cane is a backup. Her first attempts will be with BJ 9 so that she can stay away from him and remain undetected, especially by him.

With weary stutter steps, drooping shoulders, and a heavy heart she moves into her assignment. She takes a taxi to the Senate house area, proceeds with her plan, and locates where the odds tell her that the Sen. should be walking in this area very soon. She is correct. In a little while, she sees him walking away from her. She strides forward. All her training is now essential. Training is always performed in the hope that it will execute precisely when extreme mental pressure occurs. She is in trouble. She is nervous. Her head is pounding. The environment is slowly circling around. She moves into striking distance. She raises her arm to aim the dart and releases the trigger. The gas cartridge pops. The dart is on its way. The Senator keeps walking. A man passing the Senator takes a few steps past the Senator, stumbles and falls. He is dead. "Oh fuck," I missed. She looks at the dead body, "There's two bodies lying in there. It can't be. "Oh shit, the world is double. There's two of everything." Nausea is setting in. The world is double vision.

The street is now swaying. She is wobbling and bumping into people passing by. The street, the sky and the buildings are closing in as if to crush her. "I have to make one more try." She reloads her BG 9. Tries to steady her arm. With wobbling arm, she presses the button. The dart is released and an advertising balloon deflates. Missed again. By now, she realizes she is in serious trouble. She aborts the mission. Stumbling, she makes it to the dumpster and deposits the cane and the BG 9 in the dumpster.

She collapses on the street. Some people, in fact many of them, step over her thinking she is just a drunk.

THE CON MAN

MATH WHIZ

"What do you mean you have a 137 IQ? You don't look like a genius."

"What does a genius look like?" responds Brehtt.

"You look normal," she responds. "You look like a guy in here to impress us women and try and take us home to bed."

"That would be nice, but you ladies are not that type of women."

"How do you know that?"

> *"Here's where I turn their argument around in a circle. Let's see their reaction."*

"Because you look like normal ladies."

There is a pause of surprise, they start to laugh, and one of them says, "Well, your IQ just went up to 65."

"Thanks."

"Now Mr. IQ, show us your intelligence."

"Take that napkin and write a large number of at least 20 digits. Any number will do."

The number is written down and shown to Brehtt.

"Is that number divisible by four?"

"I don't know. It is just any number like you ask."

"Giving it a quick scan it is not divisible by four. But I can change it so it is divisible by four."

Brehtt takes the number and adds a 2 and an 8 to the end of the number. A 28 to the end.

"Now it is divisible by four."

"How do you know?"

"Damn it, I told you I am a genius, now figure it out."

She takes the pen and starts to figure it long hand. One of her friends says hold it, reaches into her purse and pulls out her phone and uses the calculator.

"He's right."

"Anymore tricks?"

"Try this. Can you say fifty words in 20 seconds that do not contain the letter A?

They all try but all fail."

"Show us."

"I can't. It's the rule of the magician. Never reveal your secret."

"That's a cop-out." They laugh then fall silent.

The silence is broken when one of them says, "If you can do it, I will go home with you."

"I will do it but you must keep your promise."

"One, two, three, four . . ." and on till the twenty seconds is up.

"Are you satisfied now?"

They scowl at him. It was so easy they are somewhat embarrassed and then they giggle and laugh.

"Ladies, if you do this on someone just remember that no number from one to nine hundred ninety-nine has an A in it. Just never, say the word 'and' like in one hundred and one. Just say one hundred one. If you stay under one hundred you are pretty safe.

"Well, I guess I play the martyr. Let's go magi."

"I was just kidding. You don't have to come home with me. I do not want you to be a martyr."

"If you are that good with the mind, hands, and ESP let's see if you have that magic in bed."

The other two ladies look at each other and using unknown powers of ESP they say, "Sounds good. We're going with you."

"Sorry, ladies but I must go. I hope we meet again soon."

MORE HISTORY

Brehtt wakes up, rolls over, grabs his history of cons book, and reads.

One of the big swindles was the Sir Francis Drake fortune. Ever since Drake died, cons were devising scams to get people to invest in getting the fortunes Drake took from the Spanish. The defrauding even made its way to America were elaborate plans were again laid. The cons made good money but most of them were eventually jailed.

Here's a quick one. When a construction crew cut through half a hillside near Yonkers N.Y. four men realized something big. They immediately printed hundreds of gold-stock certificates. They then bussed marks to the site while the excavating machinery was silent. They convinced the marks that the hillside was intended to uncover rare minerals like gold. Before the work started on Monday, they had sold 130,000 dollars in investments, bogus investments.

One guy bought the info booth at Grand Central Station to convert it into a fruit stand. Police whisked him off quickly when he tried to set up shop.

Another guy bought Cleveland's Brookside Park, lagoon and zoo. His enterprise did not last long.

In the 1800s, the New York Lotteries were rigged. The court acquitted the con guy. Washington, D.C. also had their rigged lotteries and even refused to make some payments.

Can you learn when being fleeced? Allen Jones was a wealthy man who was cleaned of all by a con. Jones was so impressed that he gets to apprentice with the con. He learns so good he goes off on his own and becomes very wealthy again.

THE GREAT IMPOSTER

The Great Impostor is the true story of an impostor named Ferdinand Waldo Demara. Tony Curtis played him in the movie, "The Great Imposter." The movie was based on the book with the same name by Robert Crichton. The book was able to go into so much more detail than the movie.

> *"I saw that movie, it was great. This guy was maybe one of the all-time imposters. He just conned his way into various jobs. He never harmed anyone nor did he steal money from anyone. He hurt no one. In fact, people loved him because he was so good at what he did. He just wanted a job and an adventure. This is my type of guy."*

Demara, known locally as "Fred", was born in Lawrence, Massachusetts in 1921. He ran away from home at the age of sixteen to join Cistercian monks in Rhode Island. He stayed for several years and then joined the U.S. Army in 1941.

In 1941, he wanted to join the Army as an officer but he lacked the required education, so he faked a set of credentials and became a U.S. Marine.

On being detected, Demara faked suicide to prevent a jail sentence and hides out as a Trappist monk. After a while, he is expelled from the monastery, captured and imprisoned in a military brig. The warden and Demara become friendly and he reveals much of his life to Demara. Upon his release, Demara impersonates a warden and lands a job working in a Texas penitentiary, where he courts the warden's daughter.

While here, he is recognized by an inmate. Demara then flees to Nova Scotia and joins the Royal Canadian Navy, using the forged credentials of a doctor. He falls in love with a Royal Canadian Navy Nurse. He is sent to Korea aboard the ship HMCS Cayuga. The ship's captain needs dental work so he performs dental work. He also performed operations in a Korean hospital. He was a brilliant man. He reads the medical books on procedures and then performs the operations.

While at the Brothers of Christian Instruction, he became acquainted with a young doctor named Joseph C. Cyr. He then masqueraded as Dr. Cyr, working as a trauma surgeon aboard HMCS Cayuga, a Royal Canadian Navy destroyer, during the Korean War. He performed successful major surgeries including sixteen Korean combat casualties who were loaded onto the Cayuga. Demara was the only "surgeon" on board so he disappeared to his room with a textbook on general surgery and speed-read the procedures. None of the casualties died from Demara's surgeries. Apparently, the removal of a bullet from a wounded man ended up in Canadian newspapers. His exploits reached a newspaper in New Brunswick, Canada and this led to his dismissal. He then returned to the USA as a teacher in New England.

During Demara's "careers", he was, among other things, a ship's doctor, a civil engineer, a sheriff's deputy, an assistant prison warden, a doctor of applied psychology, a hospital orderly, a lawyer, a child-care expert, a Benedictine monk, a Trappist monk, an editor, a cancer researcher, and a teacher. One teaching job led to six months in prison. He never seemed to get (or seek) much monetary gain in what he was doing – just temporary respectability.

Demara faked his suicide and borrowed another name, and became a religious psychologist. He taught psychology in a Pennsylvania college, served as an orderly in a Los Angeles sanitarium, as an instructor in St. Martin's College in the state of Washington. Eventually the FBI caught him and he served 18 months in prison.

Many of Demara's employers were satisfied with Demara. Demara had a photographic memory and an extraordinary IQ. He had two cardinal rules: The burden of proof is on the accuser and when in danger, attack. His motivation was "Rascality, pure rascality".

Again, he assumed a fake identity and studied law. He then joined the Brothers of Christian Instruction in Maine, a Roman Catholic order.

During one of his impersonations, as Brother John Payne of the Christian Brothers of Instruction (also known as Brothers of Christian Instruction), Demara was prominent in founding a chartered college in Alfred, Maine. He then promptly left that religious order in 1951 when they refused to name him as chancellor. The college was named LaMennais college but was later called Walsh College (now University) when it moved to Canton, Ohio.

Publicity of his life actually made life difficult for him, especially in getting jobs. He became friends with many celebrities.

He had interesting philosophies. In any organization there is always a lot of loose, unused power lying about which can be picked up without alienating anyone. If you want power and want to expand, never encroach on anyone else's domain; open up new ones. He referred this as to expanding into the power vacuum.

"I call it expanding into the power vacuum," Demara proudly explains. "It works this way. If you come into a new situation (there's a nice word for it) don't join some other professor's committee and try to make your mark by moving up in that committee. You will have a long haul, and make an enemy. Make your own rules and interpretations. Do not try to gain power riding on the shirttails of someone higher than you. Find your own way.

The song "Ferdinand the Imposter" used his first real name of Ferdinand. NBC aired a drama called the "Pretender" based on his life.

Brehtt wakes up with the sun shining through the window onto his eyes. He is alert. He feels good.

"It looks like a great day, an energetic day, a little golf, some poker after the golf and a few beers and bedtime."

"What a life. I wonder if maybe I should look for a steady job, nine-to-five, a psychotic boss, rules and regulations, deadline and performance evaluations, steady pay . . . Naaaa . . ."

THE SPY LADY

"Hi. How are you feeling right now Natasha?"

"I do not know. I feel strange. Where am I? I don't like the looks of this place."

"I am Dr. Bill Sullivan. You were brought here by ambulance. You were found lying on the sidewalk near the senate building. You were taken into the emergency ward, examined and found no physical damage. You did not pass out from heat exhaustion or dehydration. Your body was in good physical shape. I was called in to attend to you. While you were unconscious, you are mumbling things in the emergency ward that showed possible psychological trauma. If it is acceptable to you, I would like to discuss some of the things you said in the emergency ward and a little of your background may have led to your passing out."

"I can't stay here. I must leave. I have work to do. I want to leave, now."

"You cannot do that. Some of the things that you said while unconscious are extremely serious. Please Natasha, you need help and help must be done now and not later."

"I'm not staying here, doc. You have to be a fucking idiot. Why do you keep calling me Natasha? You got your patients mixed up. My name is Brehtt."

Dr. Sullivan is startled by the change in a lower, more masculine voice. His mind is now reeling and thoughts are running a mile a minute. "Oh, my. . .maybe."

"Okay Brett, I'm going to give you your clothes. He hands Natasha a dress, a purse, and a blouse."

"Those are not mine. Doc, wake up. These belong to one of your other patients. I have sneakers, blue jeans and a plaid shirt. I do not carry a purse or dress in a skirt."

"This is what you are wearing when you came here."

Dr. Sullivan calls the emergency room technical staff and ask that they bring in the tape on the admittance of Natasha Romanski. In a few minutes the hospital technicians arrive with the VCR and hookups for the TV. They run the tape in complete silence.

Natasha cannot speak. She is overwhelmed. She fights back the tears.

"Natasha," says Dr. Sullivan. "I do not think you are transvestite who simply likes to dress like the opposite sex or may I say act with behaviors like Brehtt. I think your problems are more serious. I think we can help. My first premise is that you suffer from multiple personality disorder or as in the trade; now called Dissociative Identity Disorder (DID). In lay terms, you are two people in one body. You have periods where you are Natasha and you have periods where you are Brehtt. Each of you is aware of the other but because you are one person you cannot physically react with each other only through conversation. At this moment you are in bed with no clothes on and the trauma of your passing out and being here has you confused as to your identity and both of you are talking to me.

"Brehtt, where do you live?"

"Marlow Heights."

"Natasha, where do you live?"

"Arlington, Virginia."

Dr. Sullivan now surmises that they go to the apartment of their personality.

> *"This is interesting," thinks Dr. Sullivan. They both lead separate lives, but live fairly close of each other"*

"I see. Evidently you two must do well in staying with your personality for the situation."

"I would like to continue right now with a little background information to help me understand what is causing this trauma inside you guys?"

"Might just as well. We have nothing else to do," replies Brehtt.

"Is it possible you were abused as a child but enjoyed it? The emergency room staff said you made statements of leave me alone daddy, I don't like what you're doing to me. But then strangely you would follow up with statements like keep fucking me daddy I love it."

"What are you talking about, Doc. responds Brett in his masculine voice. Nothing like that happened."

"Yes it did, Brehtt. You did not know about it. It was a well-kept secret. I didn't like it because daddies were not supposed to fuck their daughters. However, I did like the fucking part. I enjoyed it. And that is why I had an extremely active sex life away from daddy. I could never get enough. The other sad part of it was you drifted from me. That hurt me more than anything."

Dr. Sullivan has now firmly established Dissociative Identity Disorder.

Natasha now opens up in revealing her history. She realizes her life is over once the Russians find out about her in the hospital. She reveals all.

She tells of being a spy for Russia. She tells of her past assassinations. She tells of her new assignment to kill her best friend and lover Senator Sloan. She cannot do this assassination and she knows not being able to carry out the assignment means death to her. "Doc… Brehtt, I am now a dead woman, my life is over. The Agency will have me killed for fear I reveal information to a neurologist.

"Natasha. Brehtt. I think this is enough for today. Tomorrow we will continue. Is that okay with you?"

"Yes."

"Yes"

Dr. Sullivan leaves and goes to his office. He is deep in thought. He is torn between having to report a spy to the government or not reporting it but giving treatment. Natasha/Brehtt is sick. She needs help, not government intervention. He ponders for the next two hours and has a solution. The dilemma: is Natasha a real live person or just a person in the mind of Brehtt? Confusion reigns.

What he is going to do is unprecedented. Two days later, he releases Natasha from the hospital. On leaving the hospital, she takes a taxi and is gone. He then phones Brett at his apartment and has him come to his office. It is here with great tact he tells Brett that on her release he watched her leave the hospital, only to be shot dead when a black SUV drove by and shot her with their automatic rifles.

Brett is hurt, he sheds a few tears but he knew this was going to happen when she revealed being a Russian spy.

Natasha is dead in the mind of Brehtt. Since Brehtt believed she was dead, he no longer could associate with her. He was free of her and it was just him now. Since he could no longer associate with her, he had no other personality in his body. He was now alone.

Brett shook hands with Dr. Sullivan. Thanked him for the information and left.

Dr. Sullivan sat down. No one knows of the killing of Natasha. Only Brehtt and him. The mind believes what it wants. He wondered could this last. Brehtt would still be a woman in man's clothes, if he so desired. Natasha was no longer in the mind. Natasha is gone.